Help with HOMEWORK

5+

MATHS

Practise Key Stage 1 Maths skills for school

AUTUMN PUBLISHING

Number line

When the monkeys washed their football kit, some of the numbers came off in the wash. Help them by filling in the missing numbers on the washing line.

When you've finished, give yourself a reward sticker!

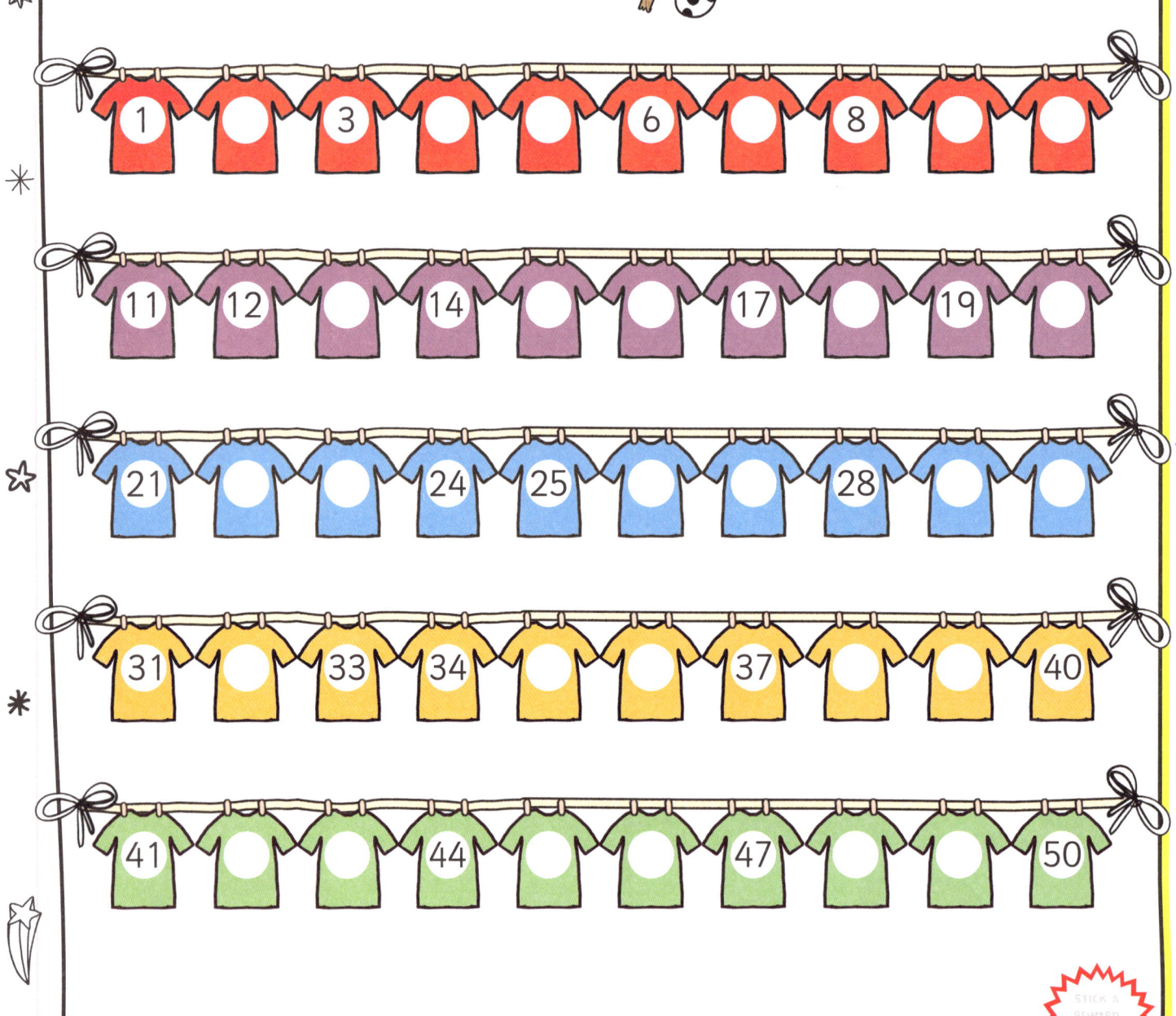

Answers on page 30

Cat calendar

Kevin the cat has a busy month ahead of him. Add the stickers of his activities to the correct days on the calendar.

March

1	2	3	4	5	6
7	8	9	10	11	12	13
14	15	16	17	18	19	20
21	22	23	24	25	26	27
28	29	30	31			

To Do:

Day fifteen: lie in sun

Day thirteen: tease dog

Day twenty-three: vet

Day seventeen: meow at cars

Day twelve: chase mice

Day twenty-nine: stand in front of door

Day seven: climb tree

Answers on page 30

3

Counting on

When you've finished, give yourself a reward sticker!

Help the flies trample all the picnic food. Count on from the number where they start to work out which number each fly ends on.

  start: 5   count on: 7   land on: ☐

  start: 8   count on: 3   land on: ☐

  start: 9   count on: 9   land on: ☐

Answers on page 30

Counting back

Belvedere the Burglar goes from house to house to see what he can burgle. Count backwards along the doors to see which house he goes to next. Write the number in the box.

1

start: 5   count back: 3   land on: ☐

2

start: 14   count back: 7   land on: ☐

3

start: 19   count back: 4   land on: ☐

Answers on page 30

Counting in twos

When you've finished, give yourself a reward sticker!

Kevin likes to jump in puddles when his human's not looking. He only jumps in puddles that are in the 2 times table. Colour the puddles that Kevin jumps in.

1		3	4
8	7	6	5
9	10	11	12
16	15	14	13
17	18	19	20

Now write in the missing numbers that match the puddles Kevin jumped in.

Can you see a pattern in the numbers?

1		3		5		7		9	
11		13		15		17		19	

STICK A REWARD STICKER HERE

Answers on page 30

Taking away

Bertie decides to burgle the castle. Complete the sums by crossing out the correct number of items, then write how many are left in the box.

1   5 − 4 = ?

2   7 − 3 = ?

3   6 − 4 = ?

4   4 − 1 = ?

Answers on page 30

Adding two groups

Farmer Freya is counting her sheep. Help her work out how many sheep she has in different fields by completing the sums. The first sum has been started for you.

1

 4  +  6 =

2

 +  =

3

+ =

Making 10

These pairs of shoes all add up to 10. Find the stickers to complete the pairs and make 10.

 = 10

 = 10

 = 10

 = 10

= 10

Answers on page 30

2 times twins

Sandra Squirrel and her twin sister Shirley have been collecting shells. They always collect the same number of shells each. Answer the calculations by writing the number of shells in the boxes.

When you've finished, give yourself a reward sticker!

2 × 1 =

2 × 2 =

2 × 3 =

2 × 4 =

Answers on page 30

Twenty questions

Time to be teacher! Draw a tick next to all of the sums below that add up to 20.

12 + 8 ☐   14 + 6 ☐

6 + 13 ☐   16 + 3 ☐

10 + 10 ☐   17 + 1 ☐

14 + 4 ☐   3 + 17 ☐

18 + 2 ☐   16 + 4 ☐

5 + 16 ☐   8 + 17 ☐

13 + 4 ☐   2 + 18 ☐

Answers on page 31

Counting in fives

Follow the bounces and fill in the missing numbers in the sequence.

When you've finished, give yourself a reward sticker!

Multiplying by 5

Lorraine the Ladybird has five spots. Work out how many spots there would be for the times table using Lorraine and her friends for help.

3 × 5 = ☐

7 × 5 = ☐

8 × 5 = ☐

6 × 5 = ☐

4 × 5 = ☐

5 × 5 = ☐

1 × 5 = ☐

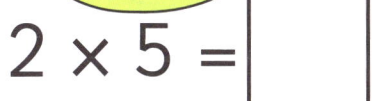

2 × 5 = ☐

Answers on page 31

More money maths

Look at the books for sale at the school bookshop.

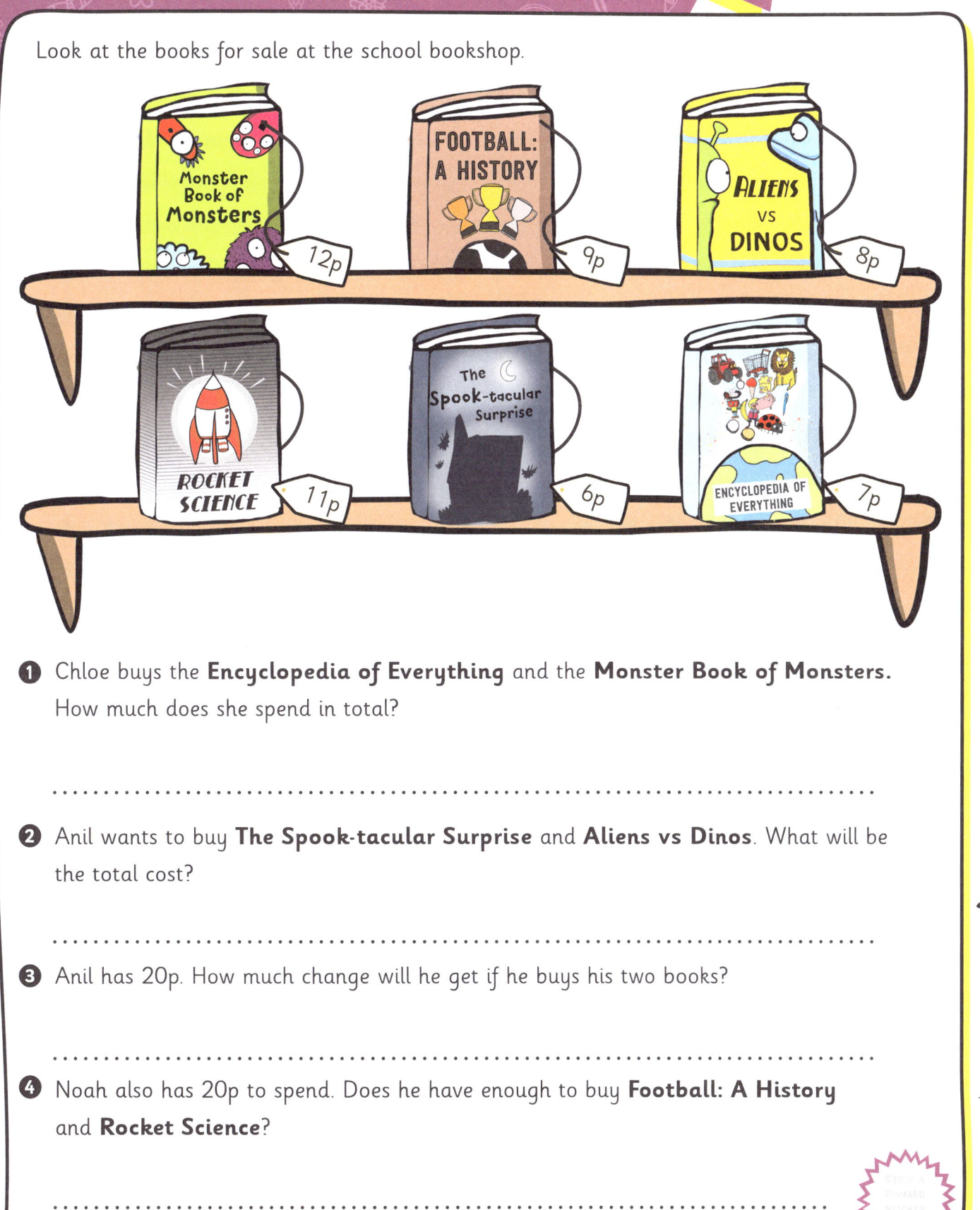

1 Chloe buys the **Encyclopedia of Everything** and the **Monster Book of Monsters**. How much does she spend in total?

....

2 Anil wants to buy **The Spook-tacular Surprise** and **Aliens vs Dinos**. What will be the total cost?

....

3 Anil has 20p. How much change will he get if he buys his two books?

....

4 Noah also has 20p to spend. Does he have enough to buy **Football: A History** and **Rocket Science**?

....

Half and half

When we split something into two equal pieces, we call these pieces halves. Colour half of each of the shapes below. The first one has been done for you.

When you've finished, give yourself a reward sticker!

square

circle

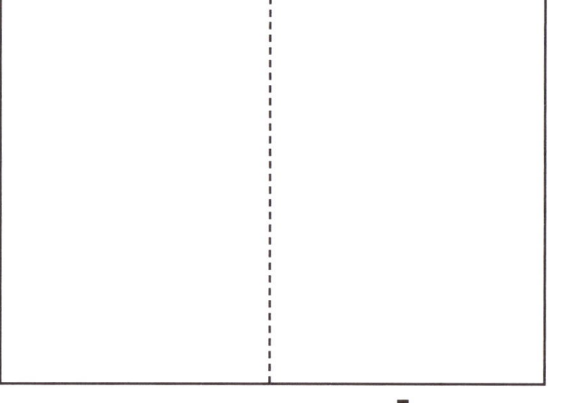
rectangle

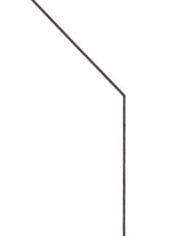

octagon

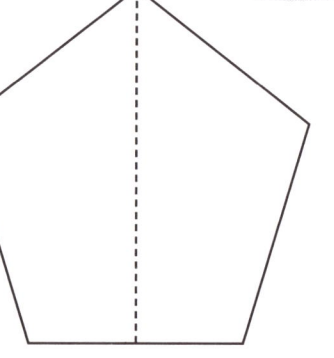
pentagon

Answers on page 31

Quarters

Quarters are what you get when you split something into four equal pieces. Shade in a quarter of each of the shapes below. The first shape has been done for you.

STICK A REWARD STICKER HERE

Answers on page 31

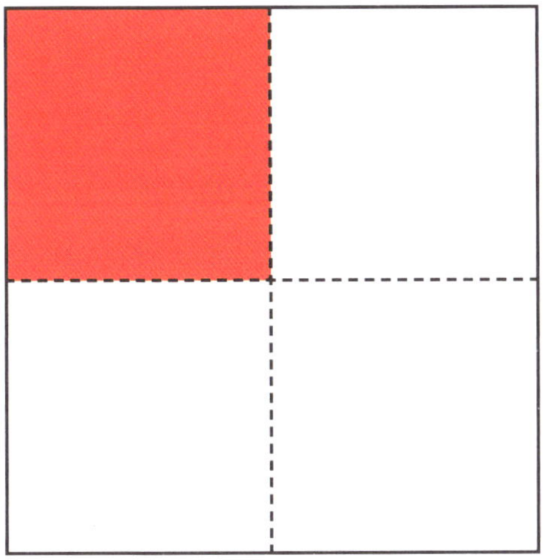

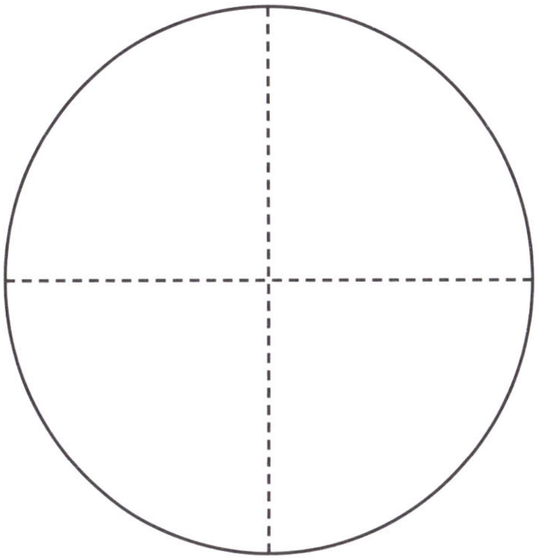

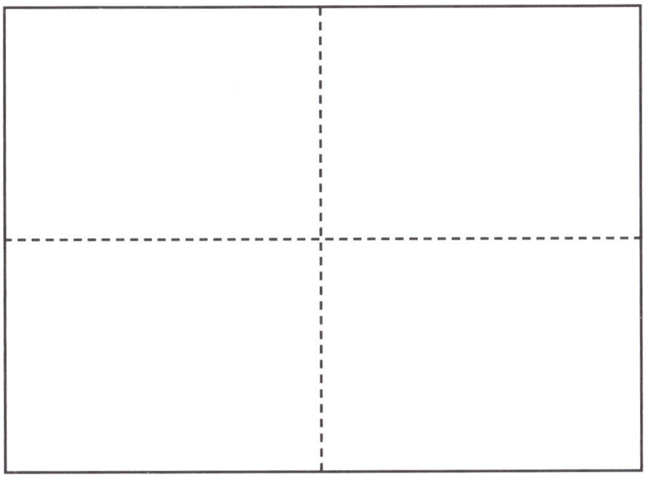

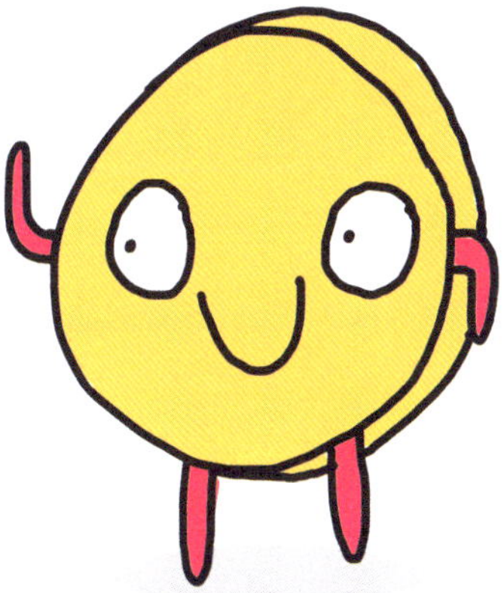

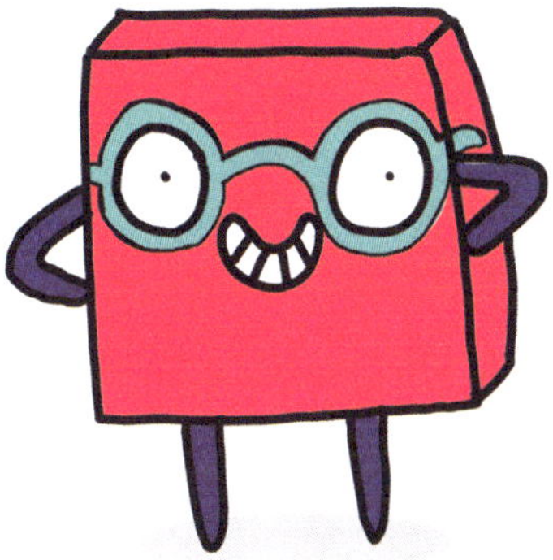

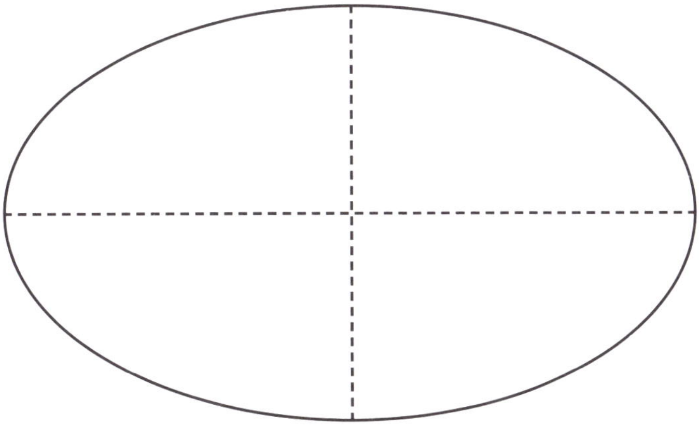

Sharing halves

The Jumble Monster has been making jam. He's sharing some with his best buddy, the Bobble Monster. Circle half of the jars of jam from each set and write how many jars he will give to the Bobble Monster.

When you've finished, give yourself a reward sticker!

1 Half of 6 jars of earwax jam:

2 Half of 10 jars of smelly sock jam:

3 Half of 8 jars of stinky skunk jam:

4 Half of 12 jars of snail slime jam:

Answers on page 31

Sharing quarters

The next day, the Jumble Monster makes more jam to share with the Bobble Monster and his other friends, the Wobble Monster and the Gobble Monster. Split the jars of jam below into four groups by drawing around each group. How many does each monster get?

A quarter of 12 jars of jam is ☐ jars.

Measuring

When you've finished, give yourself a reward sticker!

Measure the snakes below and write their lengths in centimetres in the boxes.

1. ☐ cm

2. ☐ cm

3. ☐ cm

4. ☐ cm

What kind of snake is best at maths?
An adder!

STICK A REWARD STICKER HERE

Answers on page 31

Weights

The snakes below are measuring their weights.
Read the scales to write their weights in kilograms.

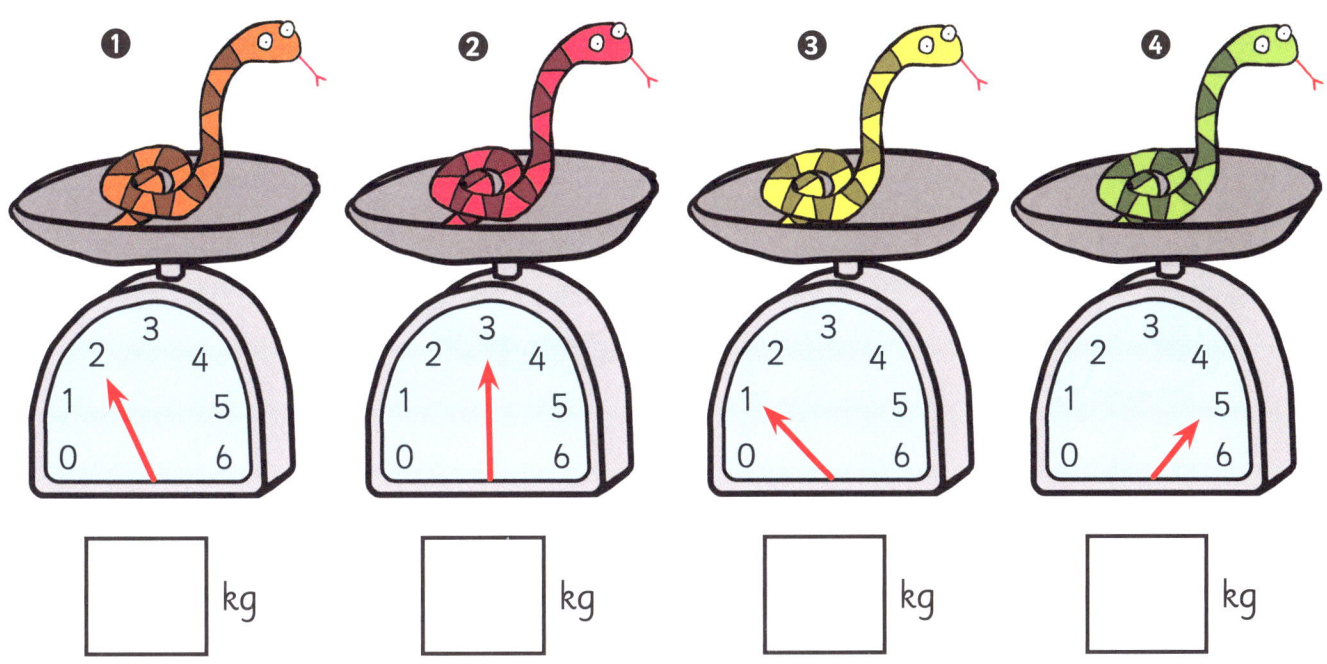

Use stickers to put the snakes in order from lightest to heaviest.

lightest   heaviest

Time

Rover is training to be a watchdog, so he's learning to tell the time. Can you write the time in words shown by the clocks below?

....

....

What do you get if you cross a dog with a calculator?

A friend you can count on.

....

More time

The cinema is showing films at the following times.

Swamp Monster .... 10 o' clock
Pirates in Space .... 5 o' clock
Super Pigeon .... half past 3
Dinosaur Park .... 7 o' clock
The Bees .... half past 9
Sharks on a Plane .... half past 4

Can you draw the hands on the clocks to show what time each of the films start?

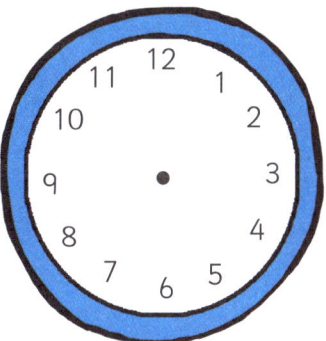
Swamp Monster

Pirates in Space

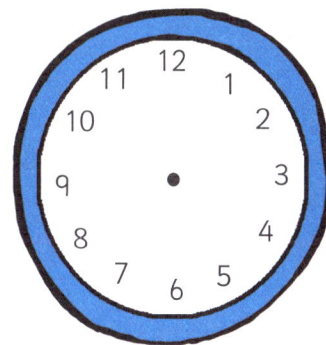
Super Pigeon

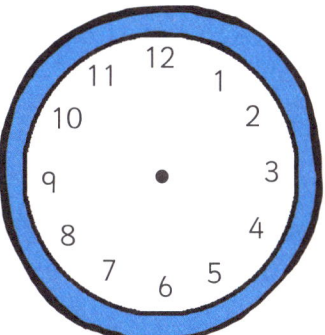
Dinosaur Park

The Bees

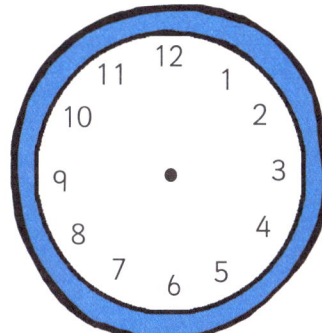
Sharks on a Plane

Answers on page 31

Turning

Pirate Sloth can't remember which island he buried the treasure on. He knows it's one of four islands.

When you've finished, give yourself a reward sticker!

Clockwise is this way!

Volcano Island

Super Frightening Island of Terror

Island of Angry Crabs

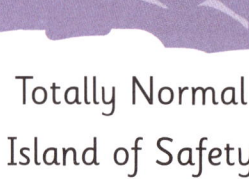

Totally Normal Island of Safety

Follow the clues to work out which island Pirate Sloth hid the treasure on, turning clockwise every time. Use stickers to fill in the table as you go. The first one has been done for you.

Start facing	Turn	End Facing
Island of Safety	quarter turn	Island of Terror
Island of Terror	half turn	
Island of Angry Crabs	half turn	
	three quarter turn	Island of Safety
Island of Safety	half turn	
	whole turn	

Which island is the treasure hidden on?

....

Answers on page 32

Pictograms

Loretta Hen is observing how many different bugs she finds in the farmyard. She makes a pictogram of her findings.

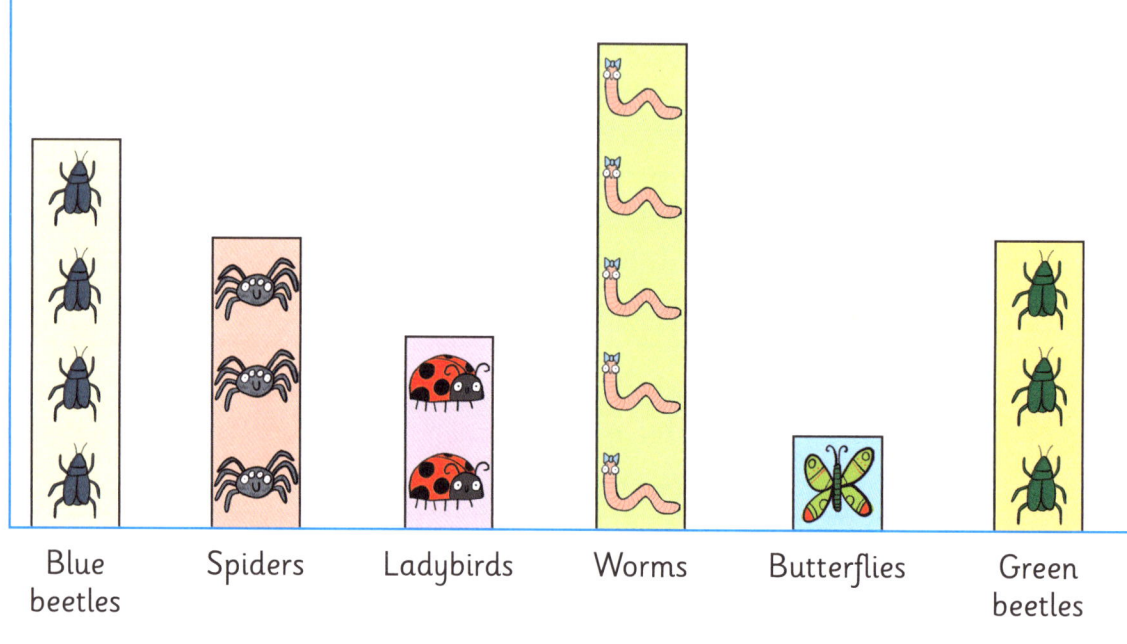

1. How many spiders were there?

   ....

2. Which bug were there 5 of?

   ....

3. How many beetles did they find altogether?

   ....

4. How many bugs were there in total?

   ....

Eric Chick also observed how many bugs he could find in the hen-house. He wrote his results in a table.

Bugs	Number found
Blue beetles	5
Spiders	6
Ladybirds	2
Worms	1
Butterflies	0
Green beetles	4

❺ Which bug did he find the most?

....

❻ Which bug did he not find any of?

....

❼ Did he find more blue beetles or green beetles?

....

Now use stickers to finish Eric's pictogram.

| Blue beetles | Spiders | Ladybirds | Worms | Butterflies | Green beetles |

Answers on page 32

Practice problems

Answer the problems below.

1. $5 + 5 =$ ☐
2. $7 + 9 =$ ☐
3. $11 - 3 =$ ☐
4. $5 - 5 =$ ☐
5. $2 \times 4 =$ ☐
6. $12 + 5 =$ ☐
7. $4 - 2 =$ ☐
8. $2 \times 10 =$ ☐
9. $9 + 9 =$ ☐
10. $12 + 3 =$ ☐
11. $12 + 8 =$ ☐
12. $7 + 3 =$ ☐

Why was the maths book sad?

Because it had a lot of problems!

Answers on page 32

Practice problems

13. 11 + 9 =
14. 18 − 9 =
15. 10 − 8 =
16. 3 x 2 =
17. 2 x 5 =
18. 3 + 16 =
19. 4 + 4 =
20. 20 − 18 =
21. 16 + 4 =
22. 12 + 3 =
23. 6 x 2 =
24. 8 + 4 =

Answers on page 32

Answers

Page 2: Number line

Page 3: Cat calendar

Page 4: Counting on to add
1. 12   2. 11   3. 18

Page 5: Counting back
1. 2   2. 7   3. 15

Page 6: Counting in twos

Every other number is part of the 2 times table. / All even numbers are part of the 2 times table.

Page 7: Taking away
1. 5 − 4 = 1   2. 7 − 3 = 4
3. 6 − 4 = 2   4. 4 − 1 = 3

Page 8: Adding two groups
1. 4 + 6 = 10   2. 6 + 3 = 9
3. 2 + 5 = 7

Page 9: Making 10

1 + 9 = 10

2 + 8 = 10

3 + 7 = 10

4 + 6 = 10

5 + 5 = 10

Page 10: 2 times twins
2 × 1 = 2   2 × 2 = 4
2 × 3 = 6   2 × 4 = 8

Answers

Page 11: Twenty questions

12 + 8 ✓	14 + 6 ✓
6 + 13	16 + 3
10 + 10 ✓	17 + 1
14 + 4	3 + 17 ✓
18 + 2 ✓	16 + 4 ✓
5 + 16	8 + 17
13 + 14	2 + 18 ✓

Page 12: Counting in fives

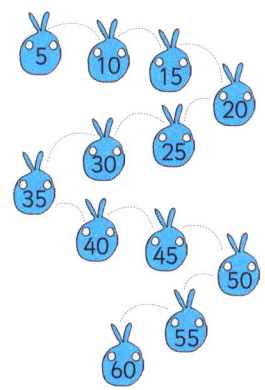

Page 13: Multiplying by 5

3 × 5 = 15	7 × 5 = 35
8 × 5 = 40	6 × 5 = 30
4 × 5 = 20	5 × 5 = 25
1 × 5 = 5	2 × 5 = 10

Page 14: Money maths

Purses with correct change: 1, 3

Page 15: More money maths

1. Chloe spends 19p.
2. The total cost will be 14p.
3. The change is 6p.
4. Together, **Football: A history** and **Rocket Science** cost 20p, so Noah has enough to pay for both.

Page 16: Half and half

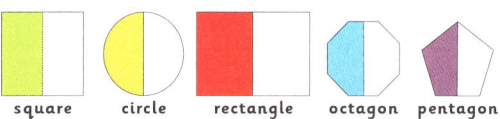

square   circle   rectangle   octagon   pentagon

Page 17: Quarters

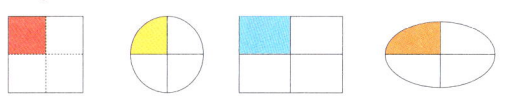

Various answers possible.

Page 18: Sharing halves

1. Half of 6 jars: 3
2. Half of 10 jars: 5
3. Half of 8 jars: 4
4. Half of 12 jars: 6

Page 19: Sharing quarters

A quarter of 12 jars is 3 jars.

Page 20: Measuring

1. 9 cm 2. 13 cm 3. 7 cm 4. 12 cm

Page 21: Weights

1. 2 kg 2. 3 kg 3. 1 kg 4. 5 kg

lightest   heaviest

31

Answers

Page 22: Time

4 o'clock   7 o'clock   10 o'clock

Page 23: More time

  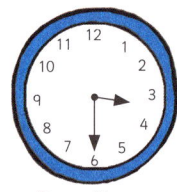

Swamp Monster   Pirates in Space   Super Pigeon

Dinosaur Park   The Bees   Sharks on a Plane

Pages 24–25: Turning

Start facing	Turn	End Facing
Island of Safety	quarter turn	Island of Terror
Island of Terror	half turn	Island of Angry Crabs
Island of Angry Crabs	half turn	Island of Terror
Island of Terror	three quarter turn	Island of Safety
Island of Safety	half turn	Volcano Island
Volcano Island	whole turn	Volcano Island

The treasure is hidden on Volcano Island.

Pages 26–27: Pictograms

1. 3 spiders
2. 5 worms
3. 7 beetles
4. 18 bugs in total.
5. Eric found most spiders.
6. He found no butterflies.
7. He found more blue beetles than green beetles.

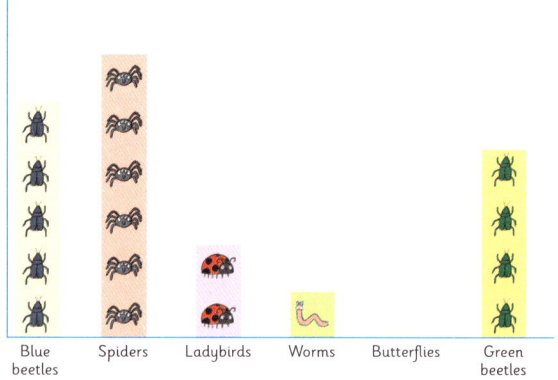

Page 28–29: Practice problems

1. 5 + 5 = 10
2. 7 + 9 = 16
3. 11 − 3 = 8
4. 5 − 5 = 0
5. 2 × 4 = 8
6. 12 + 5 = 17
7. 4 − 2 = 2
8. 2 × 10 = 20
9. 9 + 9 = 18
10. 12 + 3 = 15
11. 12 + 8 = 20
12. 7 + 3 = 10

13. 11 + 9 = 20
14. 18 − 9 = 9
15. 10 − 8 = 2
16. 3 × 2 = 6
17. 2 × 5 = 10
18. 3 + 16 = 19
19. 4 + 4 = 8
20. 20 − 18 = 2
21. 16 + 4 = 20
22. 12 + 3 = 15
23. 6 × 2 = 12
24. 8 + 4 = 12

Help with HOMEWORK

5+

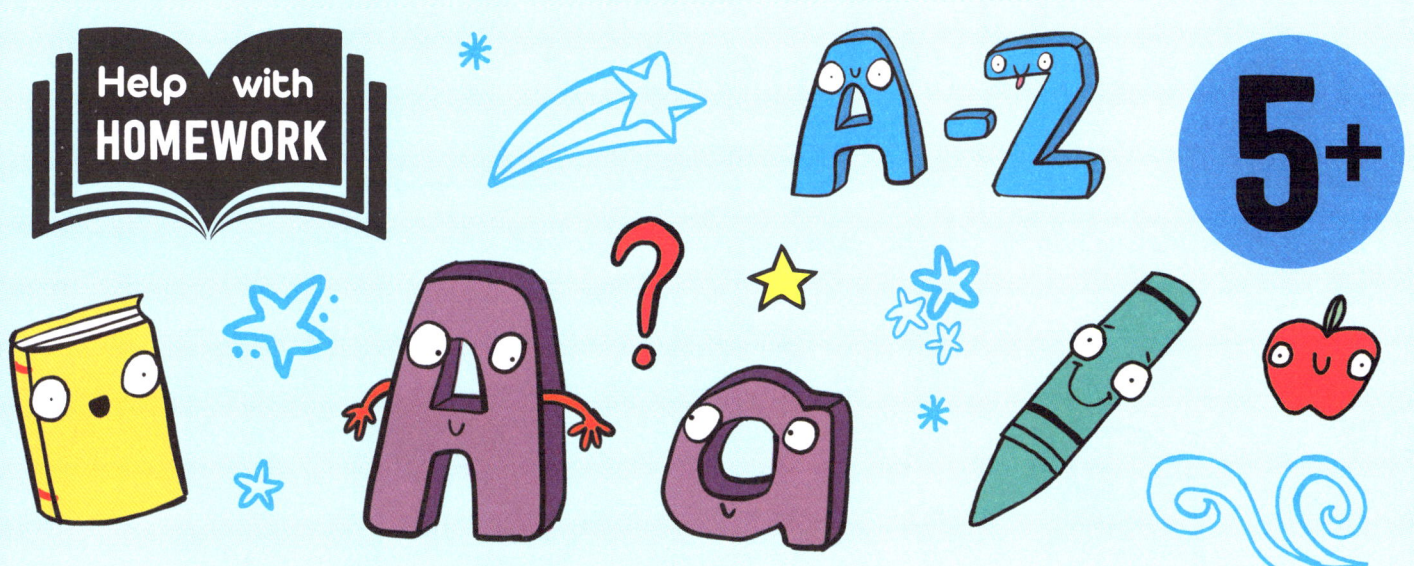

READING & WRITING

Practise Key Stage 1 skills in one big workbook

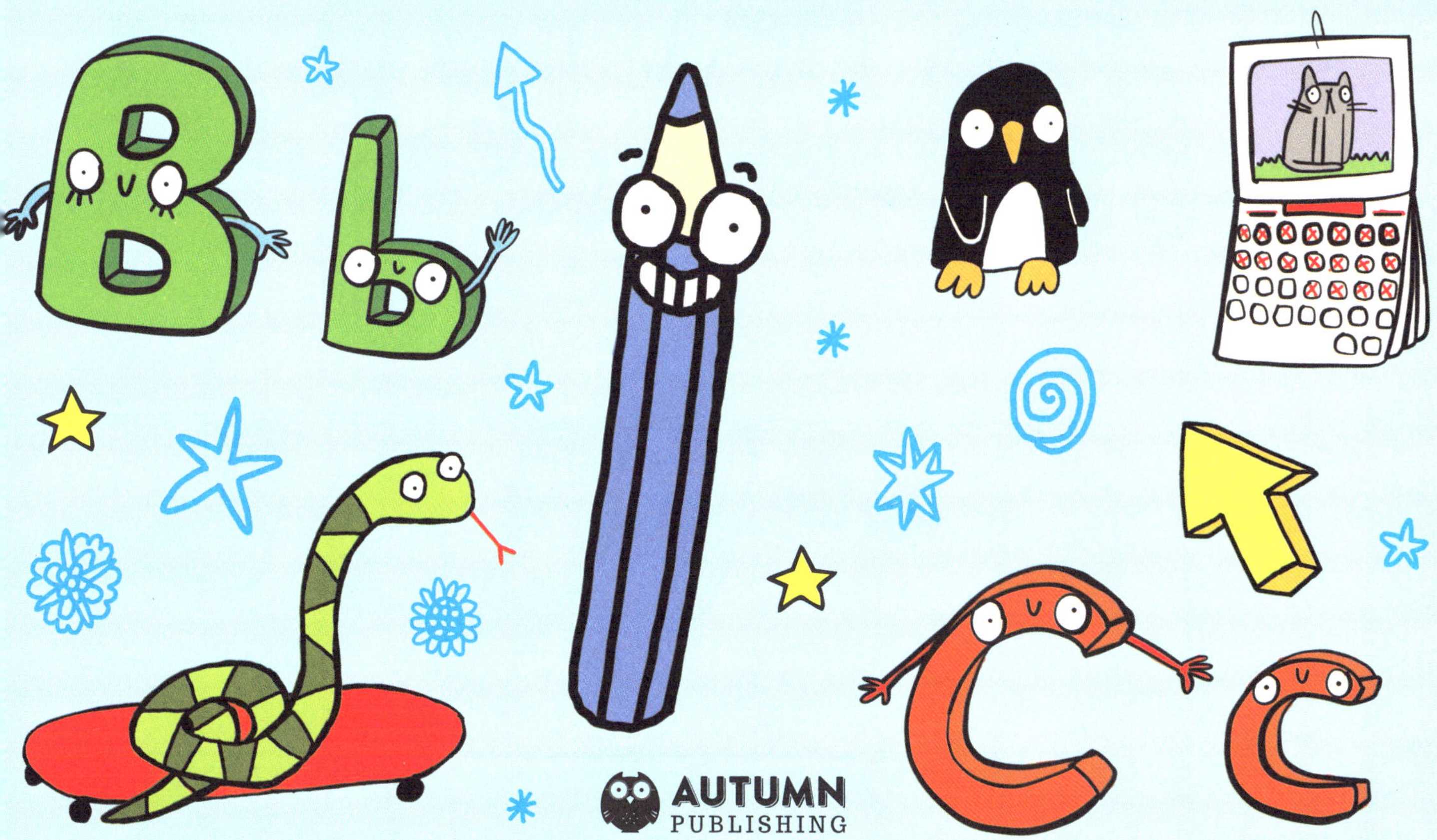

AUTUMN PUBLISHING

Alphabetical laundry

Pirate Pogo likes to hang his clothes in order from **a** to **z**. Find the letters in the pile and write them in the correct order on the washing line, crossing them off as you go. Some have been done for you.

When you've finished, give yourself a reward sticker!

n d c g j

v i m b h z

f o l w r s

k a t u q x

        e p y

Answers on page 32

Missing consonants

Write the correct consonants to complete each word. Remember, consonants are letters that are not vowels.

❶ ha__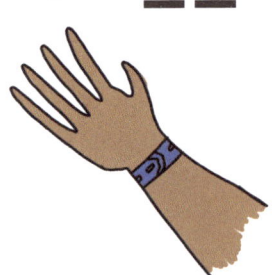

❷ te__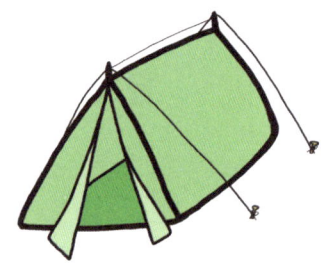

❸ __y

❹ __eep

❺ co__

❻ __ail

❼ __ee

❽ __ain

❾ __oon

⑩ __ider

⑪ __ush

⑫ __ick

⑬ __ag

⑭ fa__

⑮ __ile

⑯ __unk

⑰ __og

⑱ la__

Answers on page 32

Tricky letters

Some words with tricky letters are hidden in the picture below. When you spot them, fill in the missing letters from the box to complete the labels.

When you've finished, give yourself a reward sticker!

1

tedd_

2

fo_

3

bo_

4

5

s_ _irrel

_ _een

6

_ebra

7

rainbo_

8

ha_

9

pi_ _a

10

_ _ill

| z | x | w | y | qu |

Sentences

When you've finished, give yourself a reward sticker!

Look at the pictures. Under each one is a sentence with a word missing. Choose the correct word from the list below and write it in the gap.

snake   clock
football   apple

❶ The unicorn is eating an ....

❷ The monkeys are playing ....

❸ The .... is riding a skateboard.

❹ The .... is running late.

Answers on page 32

More sentences

Now copy the correct sentences beside the pictures below.

The snake does tricks on her skateboard.
This clock is always running late.
Monkeys are good football players.
The unicorn likes crunchy apples.

Answers on page 32

The clown's house

The letter blends **ow** and **ou** can sound the same. Can you sort these **ou** and **ow** words? Fill in the missing letters, then draw a line from each of the objects to sort it into the correct box.

When you've finished, give yourself a reward sticker!

cl _ _ d

h _ _ se

m _ _ se

_ _ l

cr _ _ d

cl _ _ n

cr _ _ n

c _ _

What do cows like to read? The MOO-spaper!

ou

ow

Answers on page 32

The crow's coat

Another set of letter blends that can sound the same are **oa** and **ow**. Fill in the gaps in the words, then sort the objects into the table by writing their names in the correct column.

r_ _d

sn_ _man

c_ _t

t_ _d

cr_ _

oa	ow
....	....
....	....
....	....
....	....

Answers on page 32

11

The bee's knees

Do you remember what sounds the digraphs **ee**, **oo** and **or** make? Use the picture clues to find 10 words with these sounds in the grid below.

When you've finished, give yourself a reward sticker!

①
②
③
④
⑩

t	o	s	t	o	r	m	t
b	o	h	r	m	k	o	n
a	e	r	e	b	o	o	k
l	t	e	t	a	b	n	i
l	c	r	t	o	r	d	l
o	n	e	e	l	i	c	b
o	k	s	f	e	e	s	e
n	t	o	r	c	h	n	e
d	i	d	o	o	r	i	s

⑤ (door)
⑥
⑦
⑧
⑨

Answers on page 32

12

Crossword

The letter blends **er**, **ir** or **ur** can all make the same sound. Use the picture clues to fill in the crossword.

Across

3.

4.

6.

8.

Down

1.

2.

5.

7.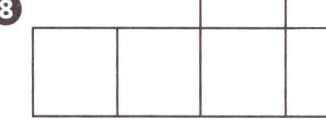

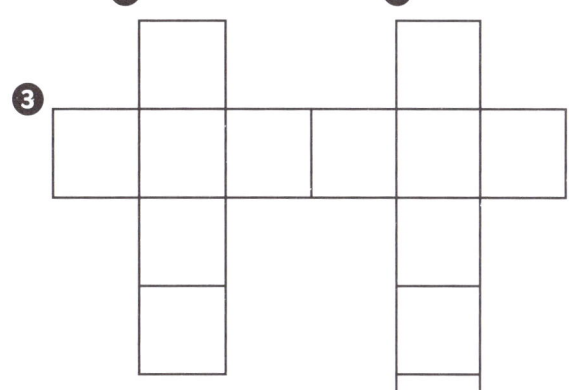

Answers on page 32

Say it again

This story is missing all its **ay** sounds. Write the missing letters in the gap, choosing the correct spelling from the letter blends **ay** and **ai**.

ay   **ai**

One r......ny Tuesd......, Burglar Bruce was on his w...... to the bank. He spotted a house with its door open.

"M......be there is something I can steal," he said. He crept inside and saw a pile of m......l.

"Hurr......! Crime alw......s p......s," Bruce said. He picked up the m......l. As he did, he hit a vase.

The vase sw......ed, then fell on the dog's t......l! The dog yelped and a baby began to w......l. "Uh oh!" said Bruce. He ran away and bumped into a policeman who had heard the w......ling.

"You ag......n!" the policeman said in dism....... "You're going to j......l."

Imaginary magic

Answer these questions as though you're a magical witch or wizard!

My magic name is ....

What kind of magic pet would you have? ....

My magic pet would be called ....

What would your pet help you do?

....

....

....

What would be the name of your spell?

....

What magical ingredients would you need?

....

....

....

What would the spell do?

....

....

....

Capital letters

Words that are the names of people, places or days of the week are given capital letters. These words are called proper nouns. Look at the words below and circle the ones that should have capital letters.

When you've finished, give yourself a reward sticker!

lola

jamaica

dolphin

ship

mars

france

scotland

marcus

whales

wales

friday

rocket

fish

What's a fish's least favourite day of the week?

Fry-day!

Page 23

Page 25

Baby Bear   Mummy Bear   Daddy Bear

Page 29

Extras

Reward stickers

Look at the sentences below and circle the words that should have capital letters. Remember, the first word of any sentence should also start with a capital letter.

1. rome is the capital city of italy.

2. matteo is going to mars on monday.

3. whales are rare in wales.

4. polly the panda has a brother called peter.

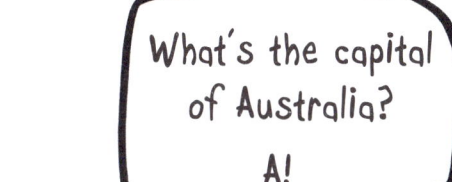

Now write your own sentence using capital letters.
Try to include the name of a person and place.

....

....

....

....

Full Stops

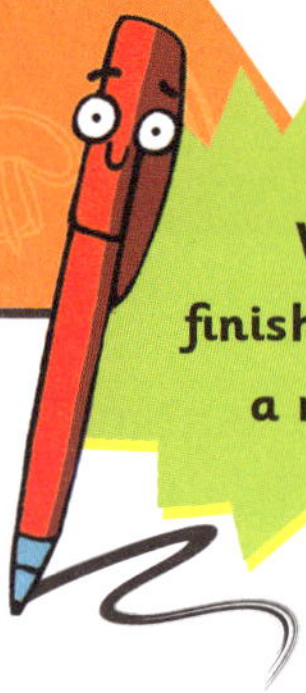

When you've finished, give yourself a reward sticker!

We finish sentences with a full stop. Arrange the muddled words below into sentences, then add a full stop at the end of each one.

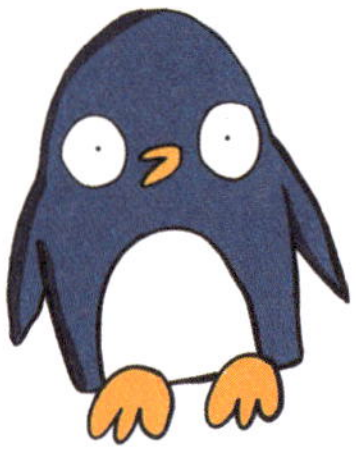

❶ live Penguins Antarctica in

❷ stairs bear The ran up the

❸ castles You Scotland lots see of in can

❹ I sisters called Polly and Newt two have

Now use the stickers to make up your own sentences. Make sure you add a full stop at the end of each sentence. Circle any words in your sentences that need a capital letter.

STICK A REWARD STICKER HERE

Answers on page 32

Commas

We use commas for lots of different reasons. One reason is when we list things. Commas go in between the things in the list, for example: **The vet saw lots of cats, dogs, guinea pigs and lions.** Don't forget to add the word **and** before the last item in the list.

What do you think happened at Indie's doggy birthday party? Finish each of these sentences with a list. Remember to use commas and include the word **and**.

Indie's birthday presents were ....
....

Animals invited to Indie's party were ....
....

The party snacks were ....
....

Questions and exclamations

We use **question marks** to show that we are asking something. A question mark goes at the end of a question instead of a full stop.

How tall is the yeti?

We can also end a sentence with an **exclamation mark** if we want it to have more BANG!

The yeti is enormous!

Write question marks and exclamation marks to finish the sentences below:

1. What do yetis like to eat

2. Let's not find out

3. What do we do

4. Run

5. It's over there

6. Has it gone

7. Eek

Answers on page 32

Apostrophes

Sometimes we push two words together to make a shortened version. We use apostrophes to show where we have missed out letters. Add apostrophes to the correct places in the shortened versions of the words below. The first two have been done for you.

1. She will → She'll
2. It is → It's
3. I am → Im
4. We will → Well
5. He is → Hes
6. They will → Theyll

We also use an apostrophe followed by the letter **s** to show if something belongs to someone. Add an apostrophe and the letter **s** to the words below. One has been done for you.

The giraffe's scarf

7. The bee___ knees

8. The rabbit___ hutch

9. The spider___ web

Answers on page 32

Weekly words

Unscramble the letters to make the days of the week.
Use the sentences as clues to help you.

Clues

On Monday I go to school.
On Tuesday I play football.
On Wednesday I go swimming.
On Thursday I go in the car.
On Friday I go shopping.
On Saturday I wash the car.
On Sunday I have a rest.

dyanoM

Monday

sueTday

Wdneesyda

uhrsTayd

yFrida

yadSurta

nSuyda

Answers on page 32

Fiction and non-fiction

Use stickers to match the sentences to the book you think they come from, then write an **F** in the box if they are fiction, or an **N** in the box if they are non-fiction.

1. Zaggy Spacedust looked the evil, eight-legged rock star in the eye. "You won't win next time, Rocktopus," he vowed.

2. The game of football is many hundreds of years old. The first footballs were made out of pigs' bladders.

3. The aliens zapped their supersonic zap rays, but it was no good! The zap rays bounced off the T. rexes' scaly skin.

4. Around the world, four babies are born every second. Babies are much like other humans, except they are usually smaller and much, much louder.

Answers on page 32

Comprehension

Read the story below, then answer the questions on the opposite page.

Three bears lived in a house in the forest.

One sunny morning, Daddy Bear made some porridge. They sat down to eat, but the porridge was too hot, so the three bears went out for a walk.

"This porridge is too hot. Let's go for a walk."

Goldilocks was walking in the forest to visit her grandmother when she spotted the porridge. She went inside the bears' house. First she tried Daddy Bear's porridge, but it was too hot. Then she tried Mummy Bear's porridge, but it was too cold. Finally, she tried Baby Bear's porridge. It was just right.

"This porridge is just right."

After she'd eaten the porridge all up, she decided to take a nap. First she tried Daddy Bear's bed, but it was too hard. Then she tried Mummy Bear's bed, but it was too soft. Finally, she tried Baby Bear's bed. It was just right.

"Zzz."

❶ Where did the bears live?

....

❷ Who made the Bear family's breakfast?

....

❸ Why was Goldilocks in the forest?

....

❹ What did Goldilocks decide to do after she had eaten the porridge?

....

Use stickers to match the bear to the description of their porridge.

            Just right   Too hot   Too cold

Now write an ending for the story. You can follow the fairy tale or make up your own ending.

....

....

....

Unbelievable 'un'

Read the sentences below. Then write **un** in the spaces to change the meaning of each sentence.

Yesterday I was the ____ happiest girl in town.

It was the ____ tidiest room in the house.

He was always ____ friendly to the other children.

The dog never went outside and was ____ fit.

My gran tells me to eat ____ healthy food.

My dad told me off for being ____ kind.

Adding 'ed' and 'ing'

Read the story below. Add **ed** or **ing** to complete the words. When adding **ed**, watch out for words that already end in **e**!

Jack finish ____ his beans and wipe ____ the plate with toast.

Then he look ____ at the clock. He was late!

Putt ____ on his gloves, he went out.

Soon he was runn ____ onto the football pitch.

After a few minutes, Jack score ____!

Everyone started cheer ____.

More comprehension

Read the poster for the fair below. Then answer the questions on the following page.

THE FUNTIME FAIR IS COMING TO TOWN.

There will be a super swirly slide, space-hopper races, twirling tea-cups, Craig the curious clown, Brenda the balloon-modeller and a strangely surprising surprise.

Date: Saturday 5th July
Time: 3pm
Place: Greenway Park
Price: Adults £4 Children £2

When you've finished, give yourself a reward sticker!

Use the information from the poster to answer the questions below by putting a thumbs up sticker in the correct box.

1 What is the name of the fair?

Funtime fair ☐   Festive fair ☐   Fun fair ☐

2 What is Brenda's job?

Clown ☐   Balloon modeller ☐   Acrobat ☐

3 What time does the fair start?

1pm ☐   2pm ☐   3pm ☐

4 How much are the children's tickets?

£2 ☐   £1.75 ☐   £4 ☐

What do you think the strangely surprising surprise might be? Use your imagination.

....

....

....

Big, Bigger...

Compare the pictures and add **er** or **r** to describe what's different about them.

Tall

Tall____

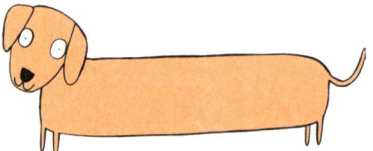
Long

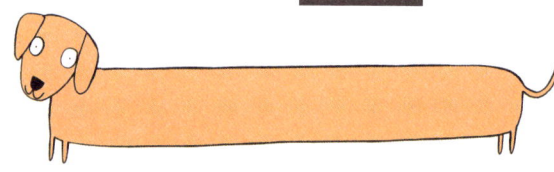
Long____

Wise

Wise____

Happy

Happi____

Biggest!

Choose which word goes with each picture and write it underneath.

Longest   **Smallest**   **Fastest**
Slowest   **Hungriest**

....

....

....

....

....

Answers

Page 2–3: Alphabetical laundry

Page 4–5: Missing consonants
1. ha**nd**, 2. te**nt**, 3. **fl**y, 4. s**l**eep, 5. co**ld**,
6. **sn**ail, 7. **tr**ee, 8. **tr**ain, 9. **sp**oon, 10. **sp**ider,
11. **br**ush, 12. **st**ick, 13. **fl**ag, 14. **f**a**st**, 15. **sm**ile, 16. **sk**unk, 17. **fr**og, 18. la**mp**

Page 6–7: Tricky letters
1. tedd**y**, 2. fo**x**, 3. bo**x**, 4. **qu**een, 5. s**qu**irrel,
6. **z**ebra, 7. rainbo**w**, 8. ha**y**, 9. pi**zz**a, 10. **qu**ill

Page 8: Sentences
1. The unicorn is eating an **apple**.
2. The monkeys are playing **football**.
3. The **snake** is riding a skateboard.
4. The **clock** is running late.

Page 9: More sentences
1. The clock is always running late.
2. The snake does tricks on her skateboard.
3. The unicorn likes crunchy apples.
4. Monkeys are good football players.

Page 10: The clown's house
ou: house, mouse, cloud
ow: owl, cow, clown, crowd, crown

Page 11: The crow's coat
oa: road, coat, toad
ow: crow, snowman

Page 12: The bee's knees

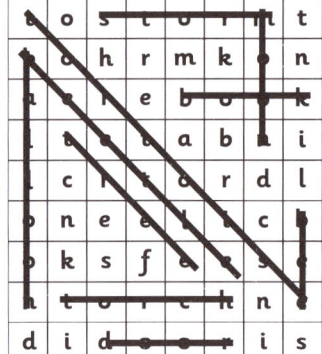

Page 13: Crossword

Page 14: Say it again
One r**ai**ny Tuesd**ay**, Burglar Bruce was on his w**ay** to the bank. He spotted a house with its door open. "M**ay**be there is something I can steal," he said. He crept inside and saw a pile of m**ai**l. "Hurr**ay**! Crime alw**ay**s p**ay**s," Bruce said. He picked up the m**ai**l. As he did, he hit a vase. The vase sw**ay**ed, then fell on the dog's t**ai**l! The dog yelped and a baby began to w**ai**l. "Uh oh!" said Bruce. He ran aw**ay** and bumped into a policeman who had heard the w**ai**ling. "You ag**ai**n!" the policeman said in dism**ay**. "You're going to j**ai**l."

Page 16: Capital letters
Lola, **J**amaica, **M**ars, **F**rance, **S**cotland, **M**arcus, **W**ales, **F**riday

Page 17: Capital letters
Rome is the capital city of **I**taly.
Matteo is going to **M**ars on **M**onday.
Whales are rare in **W**ales.
Polly the panda has a brother called **P**eter.

Page 18: Full Stops
1. Penguins live in Antarctica**.**
2. The bear ran up the stair**.**
3. You can see lots of castles in Scotland**.**
4. I have two sisters called Polly and Newt**.**

Page 20: Questions and exclamations
1. What do yetis like to eat**?**
2. Let's not find out**!**
3. What do we do**?**
4. Run**!**
5. It's over there**!**
6. Has it gone**?**
7. Eek**!**

Page 21: Apostrophes
1. She**'**ll, 2. It**'**s, 3. I**'**m, 4. We**'**ll, 5. He**'**s, 6. They**'**ll
7. The bee**'**s knees
8. The rabbit**'**s hutch
9. The spider**'**s web

Page 22: Weekly words
dyanoM – Monday, sueTday – Tuesday, Wdneesyda – Wednesday, uhrsTayd – Thursday, yFrida – Friday, yadSurta – Saturday, nSuyda – Sunday

Page 23: Fiction and non-fiction

 F  F

 N  N

Page 24–25: Comprehension
1. The bears lived in a house in the forest.
2. Daddy bear made the Bear family's breakfast.
3. Goldilocks was in the forest to visit her grandmother.
4. Goldilocks decided to take a nap after she had eaten the porridge.

Page 26: Unbelievable 'un'
unhappiest, **un**tidiest, **un**friendly, **un**fit, **un**healthy, **un**kind.

Page 27: Adding 'ed' and 'ing'
Jack finish**ed** his beans and wip**ed** the plate with toast. Then he look**ed** at the clock. He was late! Putt**ing** on his gloves, he went out. Soon he was runn**ing** onto the football pitch. After a few minutes, Jack scor**ed**! Everyone started cheer**ing**!

Page 28–29: More comprehension
1. Funtime Fair
2. Balloon Modeller
3. 3pm
4. £2

Page 30: Big, bigger
Tall**er**, Long**er**, Wis**er**, Happi**er**

Page 31: Biggest!
Your answers may vary!

 Hungriest
 Fastest
 Longest
 Smallest
 Slowest

Help with HOMEWORK

5+

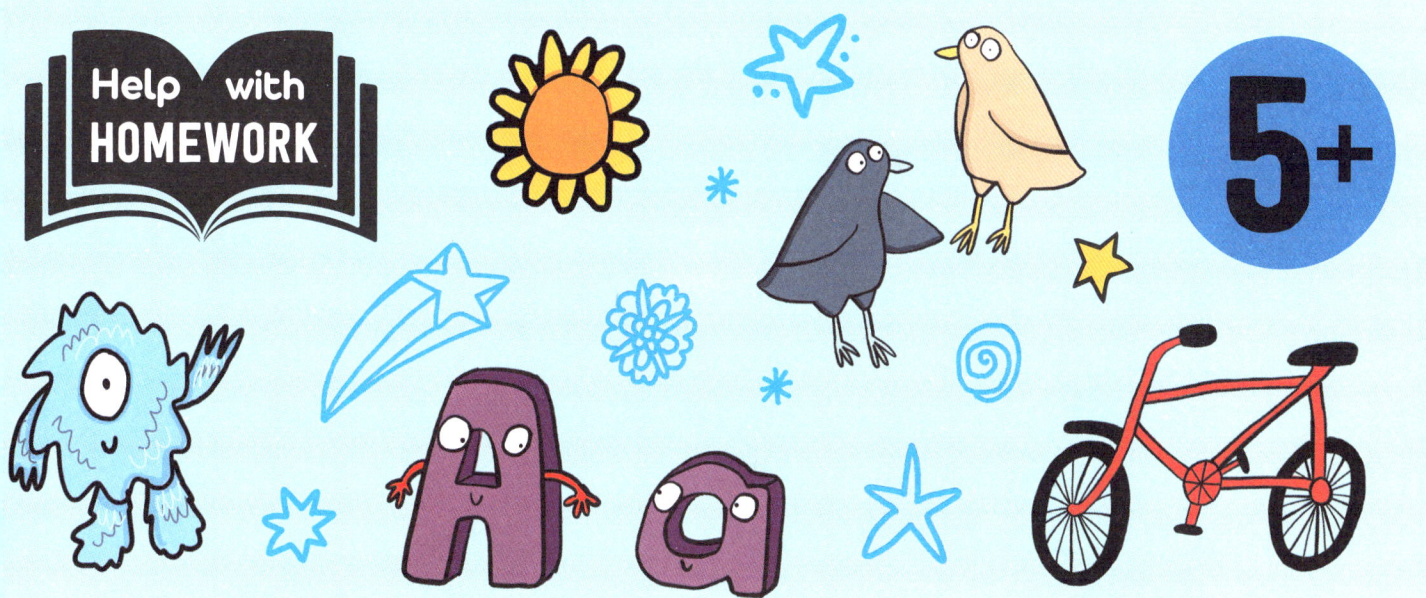

PHONICS

Practise Key Stage 1 phonics skills for school

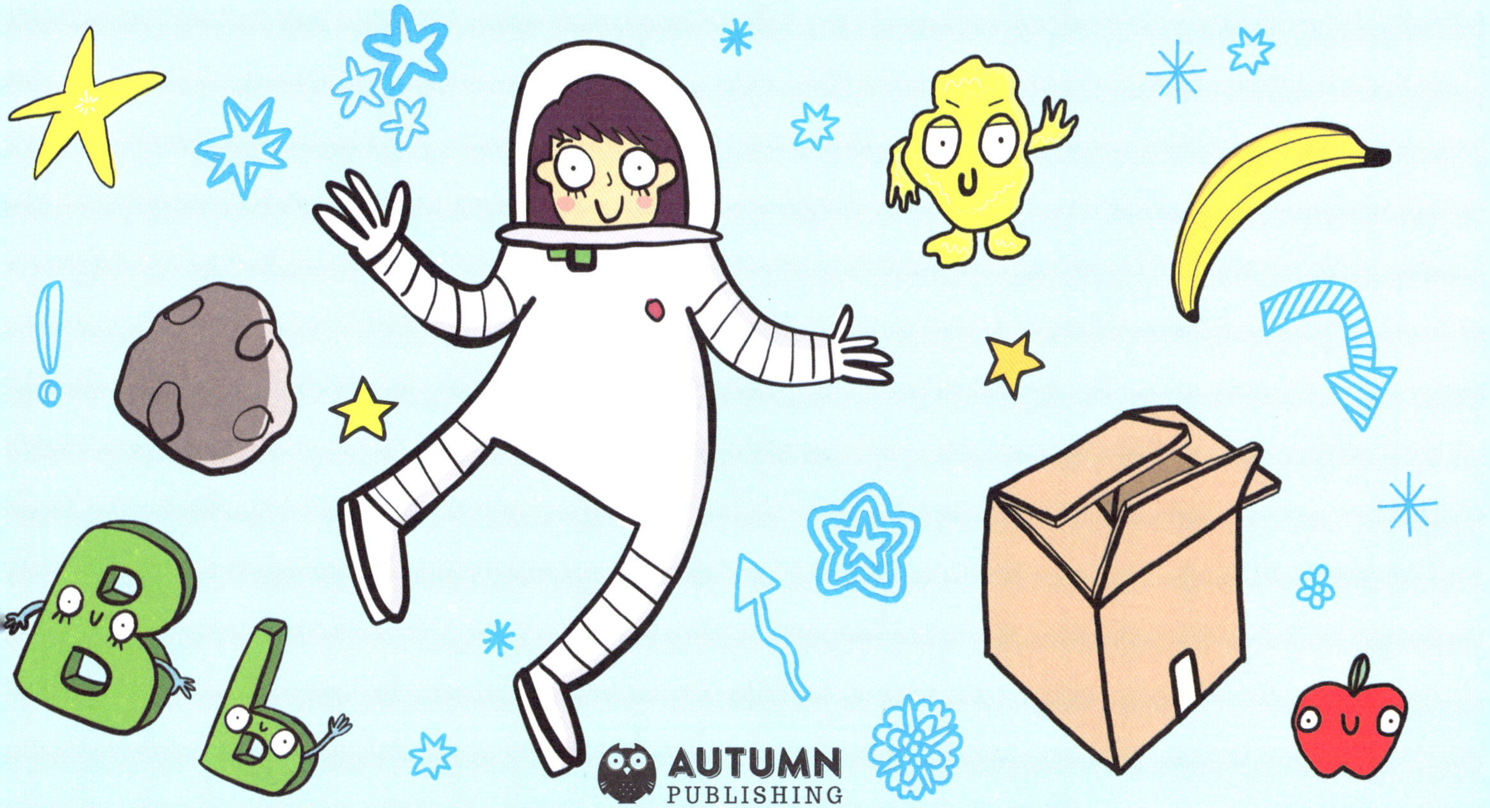

AUTUMN PUBLISHING

First letter sounds

When you've finished, give yourself a reward sticker!

Look at the pictures. The first letters are missing.
Say the word, sound it out and write in the missing letter.

__nt

__og

__an

__at

__ish

__et

Answers on page 32

More first letter sounds

Look at the pictures. The first letters are missing. Say the word, sound it out and write in the missing letter.

__anana

__up

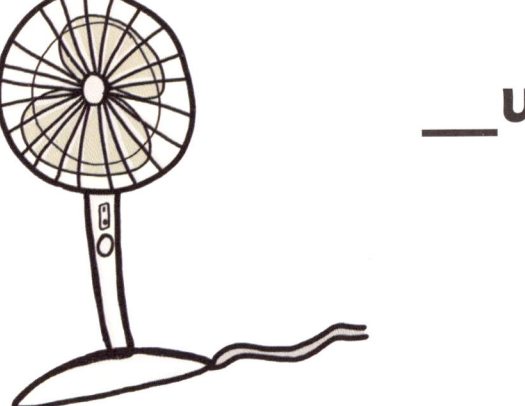

__an

__one

__ctopus

Answers on page 32

End letter sounds

Look at the pictures. The last letters are missing. Say the word, sound it out and write in the missing letter.

fro__

ja__

mo__

ca__

bir__

tracto__

Answers on page 32

More end letter sounds

Look at the pictures. The last letters are missing. Say the word, sound it out and write in the missing letter.

fla__

fo__

we__

su__

cra__

he__

First and last sounds

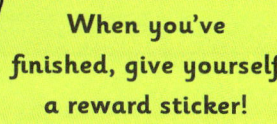

When you've finished, give yourself a reward sticker!

Look at the pictures. The first and last letters are missing. Say the word, sound it out and write in the missing letters.

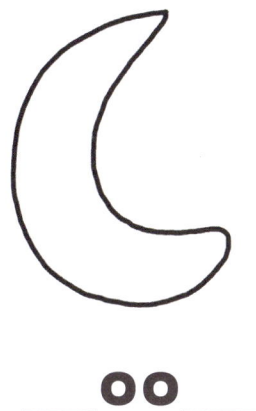

__oo__

__low__

__oo__

__emo__

__o__

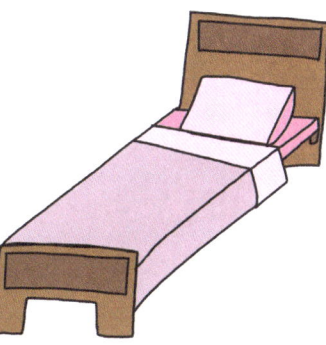

__e__

Answers on page 32

Find the missing sounds

Look at the pictures. The first sounds are missing. These sounds are made up of two letters. Say the word, sound it out and write in the missing letters. You can choose from ch, sh, qu or th.

| ch | sh | qu | th |

__ick

__ip

__een

__ink

__air

__ark

STICK A REWARD STICKER HERE

Answers on page 32

More end letter sounds

Look at the pictures. The last sounds are missing. These sounds are made up of two letters. Say the word, sound it out and write in the missing letters. You can choose from nk, ng or ck.

When you've finished, give yourself a reward sticker!

ki___

dri___

ri___

ki___

thi___

Answers on page 32

Rhyming words

Rhyming words sound the same at the ends of the words, like **box** and **fox**. Look at the pictures and the words underneath. Match the rhyming words together by drawing a line between them.

bat

clock

van

hat

king

can

ring

sock

Answers on page 32

Middle letter sounds

Look at the pictures. Say the word, sound it out and work out what the missing sound is. Write the letter in the space.

h__t

p__n

m__p

b__t

b__n

Consonant blends

When two letters are put together to make one sound, they make a digraph. The digraphs below are made by blending two consonants. Choose from the tiles below to fill in the blanks.

fr   cr   cl   pl   fl   gl

___ant   ___og

___y   ___oud

___ue   ___ab

Answers on page 32

More blending

When you've finished, give yourself a reward sticker!

Fill in the blanks with the correct consonant blends. Choose from the tiles below.

st   sn   cr   cl   gr   dr   fl

___ick

___ink

___ars

___own

___owman

___ower

___apes

Answers on page 32

Ending blending

Fill in the blank at the end of each word with the correct consonant blend. Choose from the tiles below.

ck   nd   by   sh   lk   mp   nt

fi___

du___

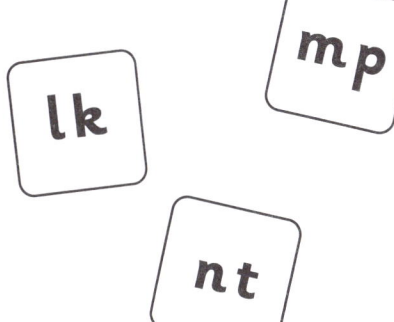
te___

ha___

clo___

sta___

mi___

ba___

a___

Answers on page 32

Is it 'ou' or 'oo'?

Write the names of the objects below underneath each picture. Which words make an ou sound and which make an oo sound?

h_____

b_____

m_____

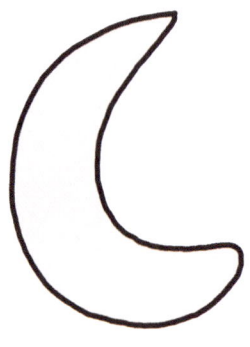

m_____

Answers on page 32

Reward stickers

Is it 'ou' or 'ow'?

Each of the objects below contain either an ou or an ow sound.
Write each object's name in the correct box, depending on which sound it uses.

ou

ow

Answers on page 32

Is it 'oy' or 'oi'?

When you've finished, give yourself a reward sticker!

Each of the objects below contain either an oy or an oi sound. Write each object's name in the correct box, depending on which sound it uses.

oi

oy

Answers on page 32

Is it 'ow' or 'oa'?

Look at the pictures. All of the words contain either an ow or an oa sound.
Write each object's name in the correct place, using the words in the boxes to help you.

a.

b.

c.    d.    e.

arrow

window

goat

soap

coat

Answers on page 32

19

Is it 'ay' or 'ai'?

When you've finished, give yourself a reward sticker!

Look at the words below. You can choose either **ay** or **ai** to go in the missing spaces. Complete the words by filling in the gaps using the correct spelling.

st___

r___n

w___

tr___n

d___

p___nt

pl___

w___t

tr___

Answers on page 32

The 'igh' combination

Together, the letters **igh** make a sound like a long i.

Complete the words below by adding **igh** to fill in the gaps.

igh

s___   fr___t

br___t   n___t

l___tning   h___

m___t   s___t

Is it 'ar' or 'or'?

When you've finished, give yourself a reward sticker!

Each of the objects below contain either an **ar** or an **or** sound. Write each object's name in the correct box, depending on which sound it uses.

or

ar

Answers on page 32

Is it 'air' or 'ir'?

Write the correct sounds into the words below. You can choose either **air** or **ir** to go in the missing spaces.

st___

b___d

f___

h___

ch___

g___l

Get Sketching

Read the words out loud, choose one from each group and draw a picture of it in the frame.

Group 1:

cake
face
snake
lake

Group 2:

mice
bike
rice
slice

Group 3:

mole
hole
stone
phone

STICK A REWARD STICKER HERE

Wordsearch

Can you find the words with **ee**, **oo** and **ar** sounds in the grid below?

d	e	v	z	l	m	a	r	k	p
a	s	d	f	s	p	o	o	n	g
h	p	a	r	t	j	k	b	x	l
z	x	c	v	a	b	n	m	q	a
w	s	c	t	r	e	e	d	c	r
f	v	t	g	b	y	h	n	u	b
j	m	i	h	k	m	e	e	t	e
o	l	z	o	p	o	q	l	w	a
a	s	j	o	w	o	g	j	d	k
s	e	a	t	b	n	f	h	q	a

tree   moon   star

seat   spoon   mark

beak   hoot

meet   part

Answers on page 32

Which spelling?

When you've finished, give yourself a reward sticker!

Finish each sentence by writing the word with the correct spelling in the gap. Remember to add a full stop!

A small animal with a long tail is called a _____

- mouse
- moose
- mowse
- mous

A man who wears a crown and lives in a palace is called a

_____

- cing
- knig
- king
- ching

When you don't wash your hands, they get _____

- durty
- derty
- birty
- dirty

Answers on page 32

An animal with a long trunk is an ______________________

elephant

elefant

eliphant

elliphant

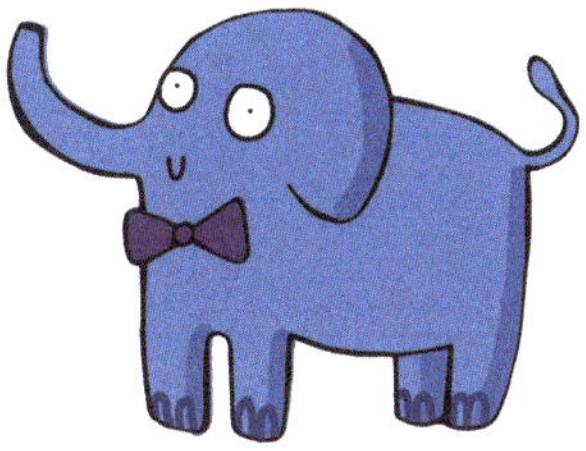

Someone who lives on a farm is a ______________________

pharmer

farmer

former

fermer

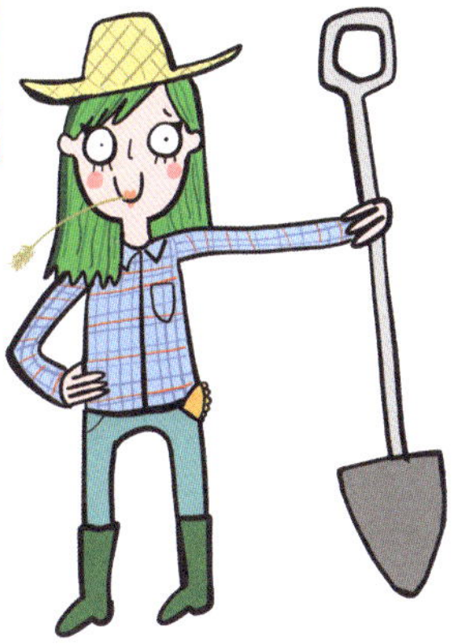

When you are walking in the country, you must follow the

____

path

pash

patch

parf

STICK A REWARD STICKER HERE

Answers on page 32

You're the teacher!

When you've finished, give yourself a reward sticker!

Look at the sentences below. Which are correct? Give them a ✓ if they are correct. If you find any mistakes, circle them and write the correct word beneath.

a. The nurse was very noysy.

b. Our garden has a lot of trees. There are also a lot of birds.

c. Once upon a time there was a Prinsess.

d. Five yeers ago, we moved to Scotland.

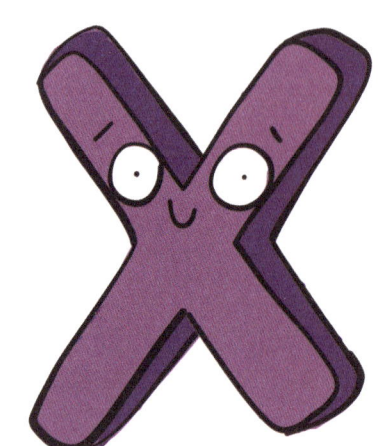

e. Wen will it be time to go home?

Answers on page 32

Nonsense words

Using the consonant pairs below and some vowels, make up some nonsense words that could describe a fruit. You might describe how they look, taste, smell or feel.

E.g. That apple smells **flurpy** or that pear tastes **glucky**!

More nonsense words

Circle the words below that are nonsense words. Then, pick your favourite nonsense word and draw a picture of how you imagine it might look in the frame opposite.

robot

kear

vurk

queen

boot

kite

chick

queck

thorden

jigh

zurd

coat

duck

nud

kitten

flurp

plab

Answers

Pages 2-3: First letter sounds
<u>a</u>nt, <u>p</u>an, <u>d</u>og, <u>f</u>ish, <u>n</u>et, <u>r</u>at, <u>b</u>oot, <u>c</u>ap, <u>e</u>gg, <u>t</u>ent, <u>s</u>un, <u>p</u>enguin

Page 4: More first letter sounds
<u>b</u>anana, <u>f</u>an, <u>c</u>up, <u>b</u>one, <u>o</u>ctopus

Page 5: End letter sounds
ja<u>r</u>, fro<u>g</u>, mo<u>p</u>, tracto<u>r</u>, ca<u>t</u>, bir<u>d</u>

Page 6: More end letter sounds
fla<u>g</u>, we<u>b</u>, fo<u>x</u>, su<u>n</u>, he<u>n</u>, cra<u>b</u>

Page 7: First and last sounds
<u>moon</u>, <u>clown</u>, <u>book</u>, <u>lemon</u>, <u>box</u>, <u>bed</u>

Page 8: Find the missing sounds
<u>ch</u>ick, <u>sh</u>ip, queen, <u>th</u>ink, <u>ch</u>air, <u>sh</u>ark

Page 9: More end letter sounds
ki<u>ng</u>, dri<u>nk</u>, ri<u>ng</u>, ki<u>ck</u>, thi<u>nk</u>

Pages 10-11: Rhyming words
bat - hat, clock - sock, van - can, king - ring, mug - rug, pen - ten, frog - dog, toy - boy

Page 12: Middle letter sounds
h<u>a</u>t, p<u>i</u>n, m<u>o</u>p, b<u>a</u>t, b<u>i</u>n

Page 13: Consonant blends
<u>p</u>lant, <u>f</u>rog, <u>f</u>ly, <u>c</u>loud, <u>g</u>lue, <u>c</u>rab

Page 14: More blending
<u>c</u>lick, <u>d</u>rink, <u>s</u>tars, <u>c</u>rown, <u>s</u>nowman, <u>f</u>lower, <u>g</u>rapes

Page 15: Ending blending
fi<u>sh</u>, du<u>ck</u>, te<u>nt</u>, ha<u>nd</u>, clo<u>ck</u>, sta<u>mp</u>, mi<u>lk</u>, ba<u>by</u>, a<u>nt</u>

Page 16: Is it 'ou' or 'oo'?
ou h<u>ou</u>se, m<u>ou</u>se
oo b<u>oo</u>k, m<u>oo</u>n

Page 17: Is it 'ou' or 'ow'?
ou m<u>ou</u>se, cl<u>ou</u>d, h<u>ou</u>se
ow cr<u>ow</u>n, cl<u>ow</u>n, fl<u>ow</u>er

Page 18: Is it 'oy' or 'oi'?
oy b<u>oy</u>, t<u>oy</u>
oi p<u>oi</u>nt, c<u>oi</u>n, t<u>oi</u>let

Page 19: Is it 'ow' or 'oa'?
a. s<u>oa</u>p, **b.** arr<u>ow</u>, **c.** wind<u>ow</u>, **d.** g<u>oa</u>t **e.** c<u>oa</u>t

Page 20: Is it 'ay' or 'ai'?
r<u>ai</u>n, st<u>ay</u>, w<u>ay</u>, d<u>ay</u>, tr<u>ai</u>n, p<u>ai</u>nt, w<u>ai</u>t, pl<u>ay</u>, tr<u>ay</u>

Page 21: The 'igh' combination
s<u>igh</u>, fr<u>igh</u>t, br<u>igh</u>t, n<u>igh</u>t, l<u>igh</u>tning, h<u>igh</u>, m<u>igh</u>t, s<u>igh</u>t

Page 22: Is it 'ar' or 'or'?
ar st<u>ar</u>, c<u>ar</u>, j<u>ar</u>, <u>ar</u>row
or f<u>or</u>k, d<u>or</u>

Page 23: Is it 'air' or 'ir'?
air st<u>air</u>, f<u>air</u>, h<u>air</u>, ch<u>air</u>
ir b<u>ir</u>d, g<u>ir</u>l

Page 25: Wordsearch

d	e	v	z	l	m	a	r	k	p
a	s	d	f	s	p	o	o	n	g
h	p	a	r	t	j	k	b	x	l
z	x	c	v	a	b	n	m	q	a
w	s	c	t	r	e	e	d	c	r
f	v	t	q	b	y	h	n	u	b
j	m	i	h	k	m	e	e	t	e
o	l	z	o	p	o	q	l	w	a
a	s	j	o	w	o	g	j	d	k
s	e	a	t	b	n	f	h	q	a

Pages 26-27: Which spelling?
A small animal with a long tail is called a **mouse**.
A man who wears a crown and lives in a palace is called a **king**.
When you don't wash your hands, they get **dirty**.
An animal with a long trunk is called an **elephant**.
Someone who lives on a farm is a **farmer**.
When you are walking in the country, you must follow the **path**.

Page 28: You're the teacher!
a. The nurse was very <u>noisy</u>.
b. Correct.
c. Once upon a time there was a <u>Princess</u>.
d. Five <u>years</u> ago, we moved to Scotland.
e. <u>When</u> will it be time to go home?

Page 30: More nonsense words
vurk, kear, thorden, queck, jigh, zurd, nud, plab, flurp

Help with HOMEWORK

5+

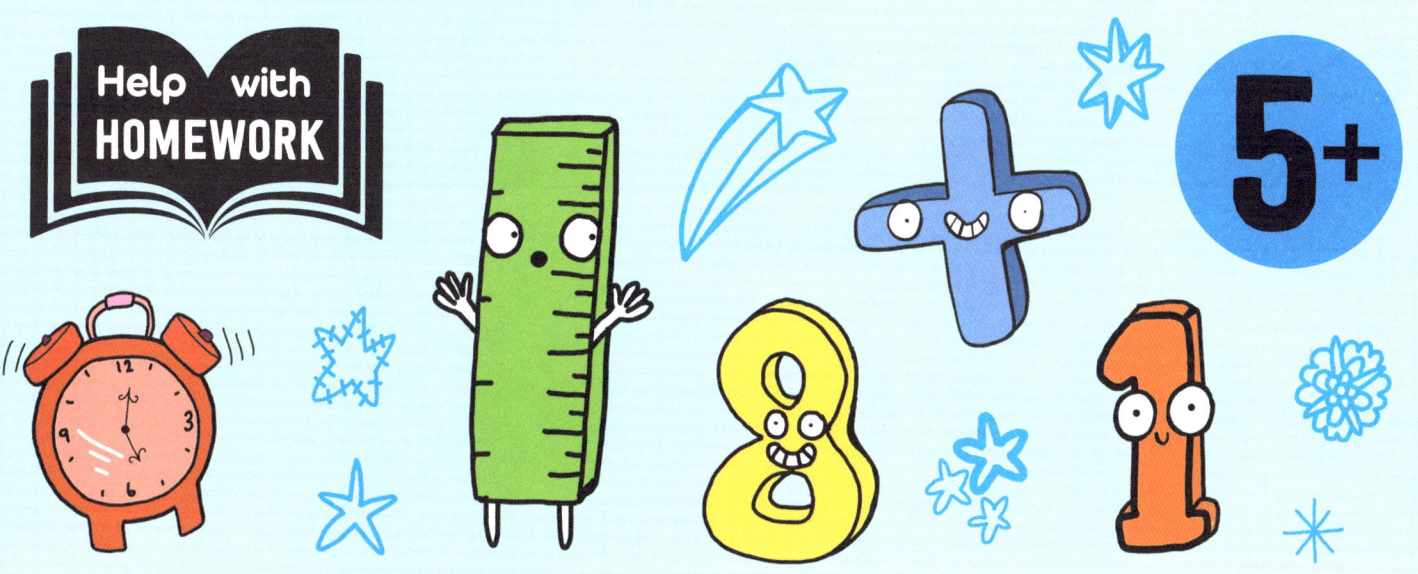

ADDING & SUBTRACTING

Practise Key Stage 1 Maths skills for school

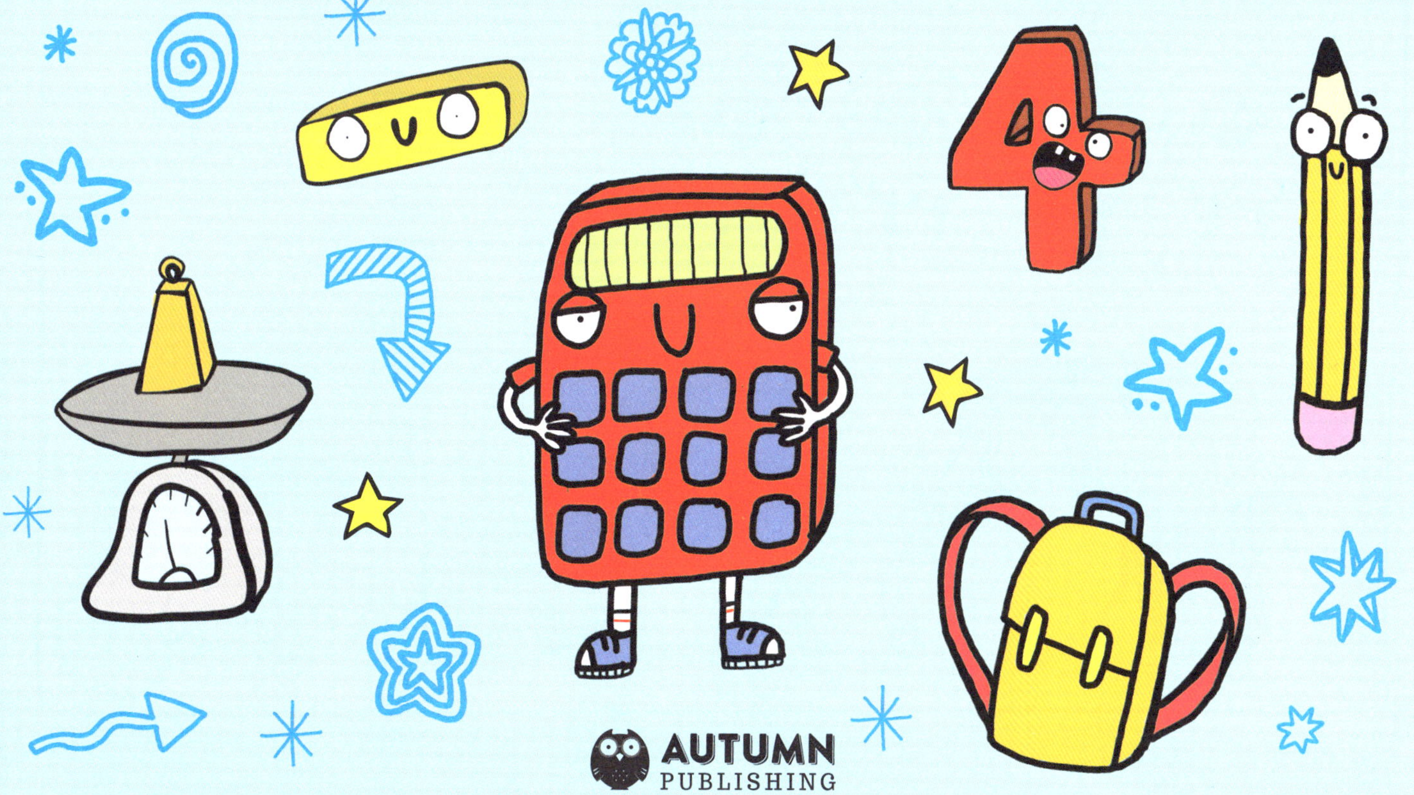

AUTUMN PUBLISHING

Counting 1 – 10

When you've finished, give yourself a reward sticker!

Count how many things there are in each row. Write your answers in the boxes.

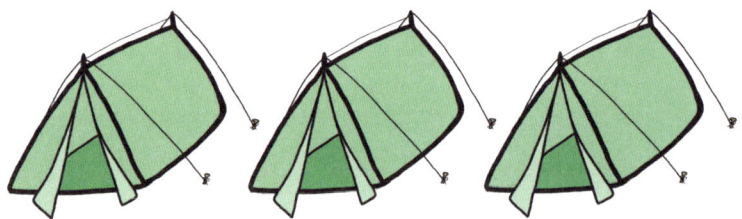

STICK A REWARD STICKER HERE

2

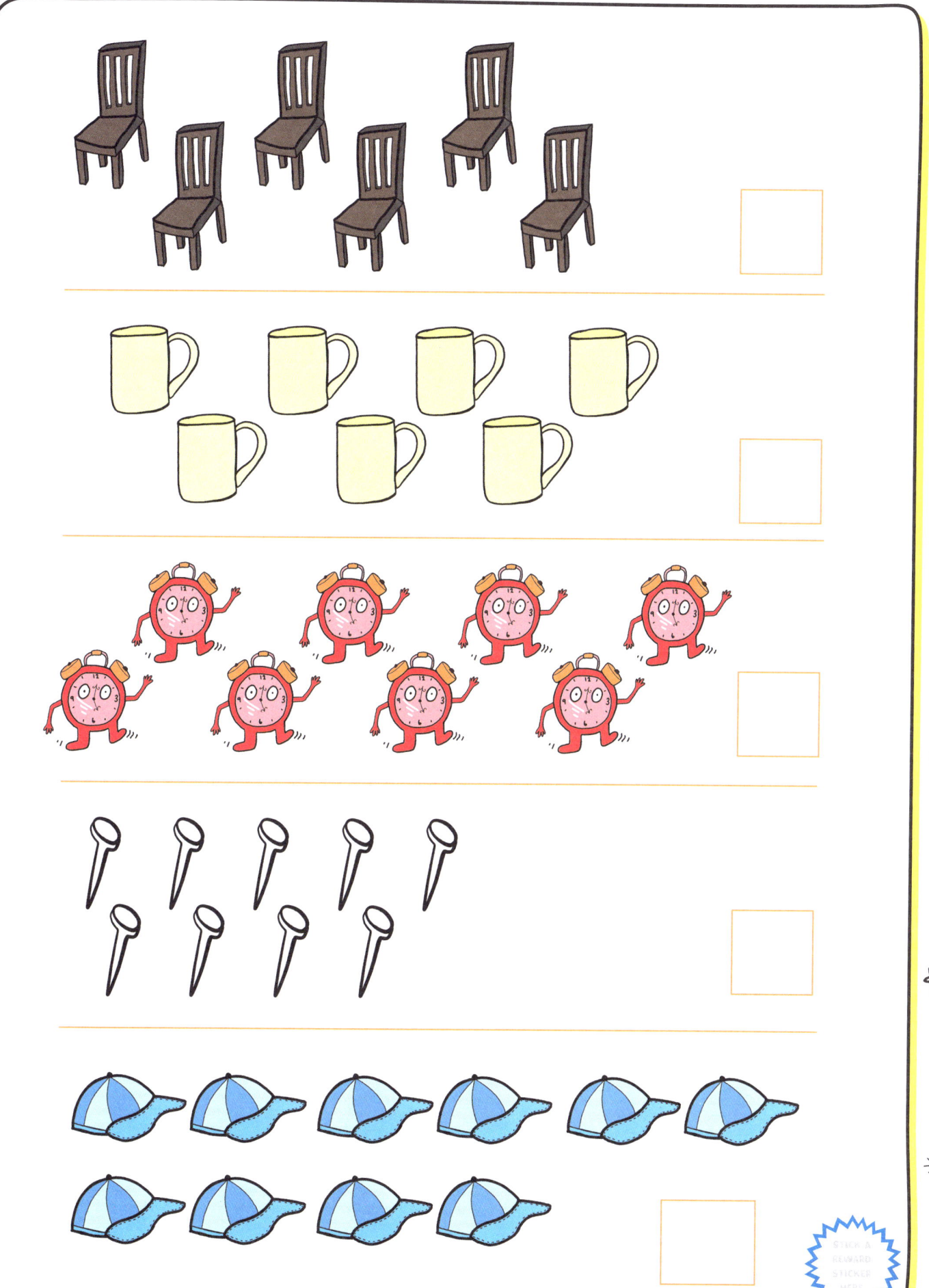

Counting 11 – 20

When you've finished, give yourself a reward sticker!

Count how many things there are in each row. Write your answers in the boxes.

STICK A REWARD STICKER HERE

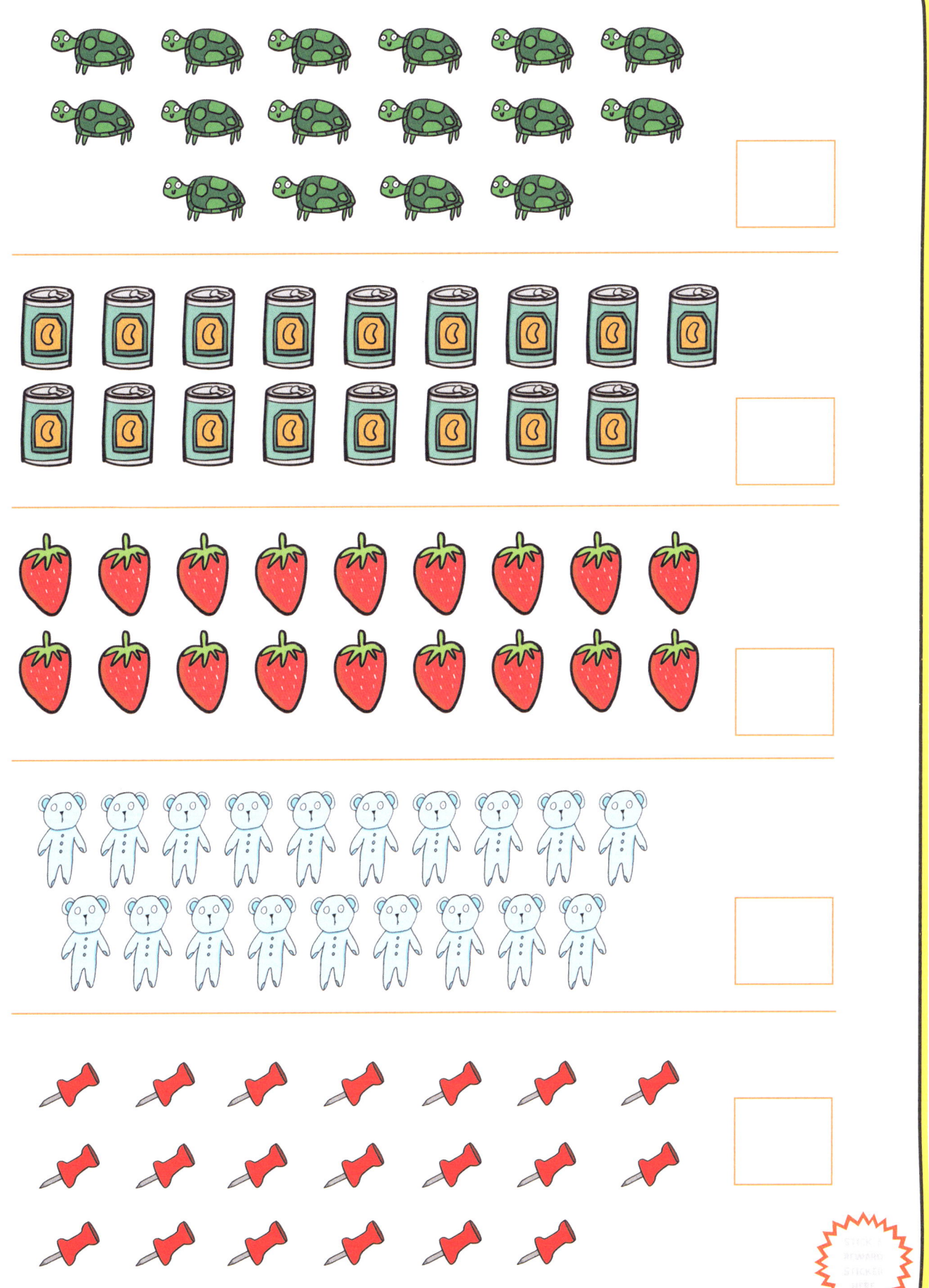

Adding one more

Using the pictures below, practise adding one more.
e.g. 3 apples + 1 apple = 4 apples.
Write your answers in the boxes.

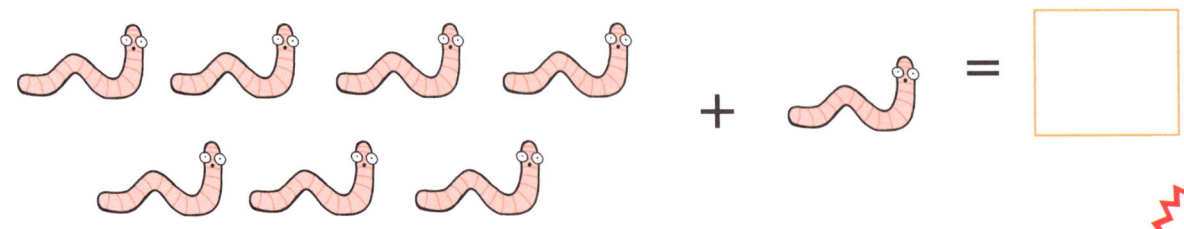

Adding bigger numbers

Using the pictures below, practise adding two, three or four more.
e.g. 3 apples + 2 apples = 5 apples.
Write your answers in the boxes.

Answers on page 31

Number bonds to 10

Solve these addition problems by adding the numbers together.
Write your answers in the boxes.
What do you notice about the answers?

6 + 4 = ☐   3 + 7 = ☐

8 + 2 = ☐   9 + 1 = ☐

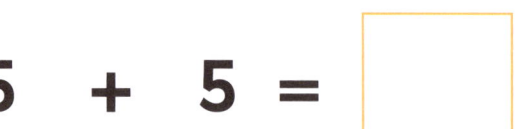

5 + 5 = ☐   7 + 3 = ☐

4 + 6 = ☐   2 + 8 = ☐

Number bonds to 20

Solve these addition problems by adding the numbers together.
Write your answers in the boxes.
What do you notice about the answers?

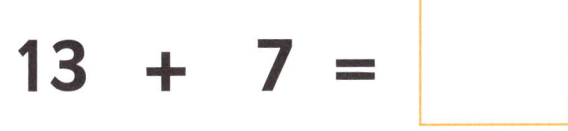

13 + 7 = ☐   8 + 12 = ☐

14 + 6 = ☐   9 + 11 = ☐

15 + 5 = ☐   10 + 10 = ☐

17 + 3 = ☐   18 + 2 = ☐

1 + 19 = ☐   12 + 8 = ☐

Answers on page 31

Super Sums

Solve these addition problems by adding the numbers together. Write your answers in the boxes.

4 + 3 =   5 + 4 =

2 + 6 =   7 + 4 =

9 + 5 =   7 + 8 =

1 + 19 =   2 + 8 =

7 + 7 =   6 + 9 =

17 + 3 = ☐   10 + 3 = ☐

13 + 4 = ☐   2 + 9 = ☐

4 + 11 = ☐   3 + 5 = ☐

15 + 5 = ☐   7 + 12 = ☐

4 + 6 = ☐   13 + 6 = ☐

5 + 4 = ☐   12 + 5 = ☐

Answers on page 31

Fact families

When you've finished, give yourself a reward sticker!

Here is a fact family for 2 + 8 = 10.

- 2 + 8 = 10
- 8 + 2 = 10
- 10 − 8 = 2
- 10 − 2 = 8

Complete the following fact families:

- 3 + 7 = 10
- ___ + ___ = ___

- ___ − ___ = ___
- ___ − ___ = ___

- 1 + 6 = 7
- ___ + ___ = ___

- ___ − ___ = ___
- ___ − ___ = ___

- 5 + 4 = 9
- ___ + ___ = ___

- ___ − ___ = ___
- ___ − ___ = ___

Here is a fact family for 4 + 3 = 7.

- 4 + 3 = 7
- 3 + 4 = 7
- 7 − 3 = 4
- 7 − 4 = 3

Complete the following fact families:

- 5 + 8 = 13
- ___ + ___ = ___
- ___ − ___ = ___
- ___ − ___ = ___

- 2 + 3 = 5
- ___ + ___ = ___
- ___ − ___ = ___
- ___ − ___ = ___

- 6 + 5 = 11
- ___ + ___ = ___
- ___ − ___ = ___
- ___ − ___ = ___

Missing numbers

Fill in the missing numbers to solve these addition problems.

e.g. 14 + [3] = 17

[ ] + 4 = 7   [ ] + 2 = 8

5 + [ ] = 9   6 + [ ] = 11

[ ] + 10 = 16   [ ] + 10 = 18

12 + [ ] = 15   14 + [ ] = 16

[ ] + 13 = 18   [ ] + 11 = 19

Answers on page 31

Seeing double

Double the numbers below. Write your answers in the boxes.
Hint: 4 + 4 = 8 is the same as saying double 4 = 8.

Double 3 = ☐   Double 5 = ☐

Double 6 = ☐   Double 9 = ☐

Double 7 = ☐   Double 8 = ☐

Double 4 = ☐   Double 10 = ☐

Answers on page 31

Subtracting one

Using the pictures below, practise subtracting one.
e.g. 3 apples − 1 apple = 2 apples.
Write your answers in the boxes.

   −  =

Answers on page 31

Reward stickers

Subtracting bigger numbers

Using the pictures below, practise subtracting two, three or four.
e.g. 7 apples – 2 apples = 5 apples.
Write your answers in the boxes.

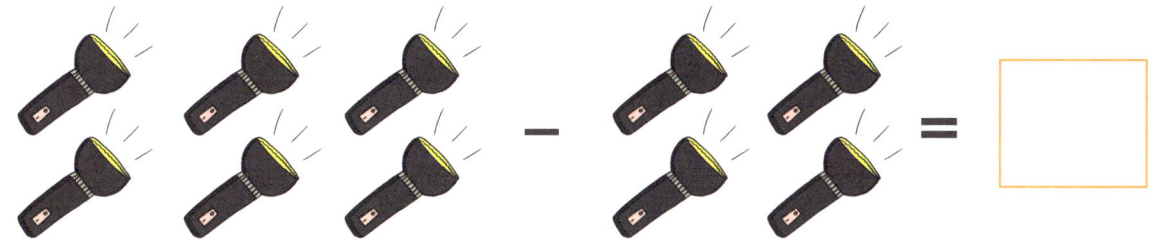

Subtracting from 10

When you've finished, give yourself a reward sticker!

Practise taking numbers away from 10 by doing the subtraction problems below. Write your answers in the boxes.

10 − 7 =   10 − 4 =

10 − 3 =   10 − 8 =

10 − 5 =   10 − 2 =

10 − 6 =   10 − 1 =

10 − 9 =   10 − 10 =

STICK A REWARD STICKER HERE

Answers on page 32

Super Subtracting

Now practise taking single digit numbers from two digit numbers by completing these subtraction problems. Write your answers in the boxes.

17 − 6 = ☐   18 − 5 = ☐

19 − 4 = ☐   17 − 3 = ☐

16 − 5 = ☐   14 − 6 = ☐

12 − 5 = ☐   13 − 7 = ☐

15 − 8 = ☐   18 − 9 = ☐

Answers on page 32

Fact families

When you've finished, give yourself a reward sticker!

Here is a fact family for 9 – 6 = 3.

- 9 – 6 = 3
- 9 – 3 = 6
- 3 + 6 = 9
- 6 + 3 = 9

Complete the following fact families:

- 9 – 7 = 2
- ___ – ___ = ___
- ___ + ___ = ___
- ___ + ___ = ___

- 8 – 3 = 5
- ___ – ___ = ___
- ___ + ___ = ___
- ___ + ___ = ___

- 9 – 5 = 4
- ___ – ___ = ___
- ___ + ___ = ___
- ___ + ___ = ___

STICK A REWARD STICKER HERE

Here is a fact family for 7 − 1 = 6.

- 7 − 1 = 6
- 7 − 6 = 1
- 6 + 1 = 7
- 1 + 6 = 7

Complete the following fact families:

- 13 − 8 = 5
- ___ − ___ = ___
- ___ + ___ = ___
- ___ + ___ = ___

- 10 − 3 = 7
- ___ − ___ = ___
- ___ + ___ = ___
- ___ + ___ = ___

- 11 − 2 = 9
- ___ − ___ = ___
- ___ + ___ = ___
- ___ + ___ = ___

Answers on page 32

Subtracting superstar

Time to practise taking away! Complete these problems and write your answers in the boxes.

When you've finished, give yourself a reward sticker!

6 − 4 = ☐   9 − 3 = ☐

17 − 4 = ☐   19 − 5 = ☐

14 − 8 = ☐   9 − 8 = ☐

19 − 9 = ☐   15 − 8 = ☐

10 − 7 = ☐   15 − 9 = ☐

16 − 4 = 11 − 2 =

12 − 7 = 13 − 6 =

15 − 7 = 17 − 9 =

15 − 5 = 16 − 7 =

14 − 6 = 19 − 6 =

15 − 4 = 12 − 4 =

Answers on page 32

Subtracting from 20

Practise taking numbers away from 20 by doing the subtraction problems below. Write your answers in the boxes.

When you've finished, give yourself a reward sticker!

20 − 7 = ☐   20 − 4 = ☐

20 − 9 = ☐   20 − 6 = ☐

20 − 5 = ☐   20 − 14 = ☐

20 − 12 = ☐   20 − 17 = ☐

20 − 18 = ☐   20 − 13 = ☐

20 − 8 = ☐   20 − 16 = ☐

20 − 2 = ☐   20 − 19 = ☐

20 − 1 = ☐   20 − 11 = ☐

Amazing subtracting

When you've finished, give yourself a reward sticker!

Fill in the missing numbers to solve these subtraction problems.

e.g. 8 – 5 = 3

8 – ☐ = 2

6 – ☐ = 1

☐ – 8 = 11

☐ – 3 = 14

14 – ☐ = 6

17 – ☐ = 8

☐ – 8 = 7

☐ – 13 = 7

STICK A REWARD STICKER HERE

12 − ☐ = 7   15 − ☐ = 6

☐ − 7 = 10   ☐ − 13 = 5

17 − ☐ = 2   14 − ☐ = 7

☐ − 9 = 10   ☐ − 10 = 8

16 − ☐ = 3   12 − ☐ = 6

Halving

This activity is all about halving numbers. Have a go at the questions below. Hint: half of 6 = 3 is the same as 6 − 3 = 3.

When you've finished, give yourself a reward sticker!

What is half of 8?

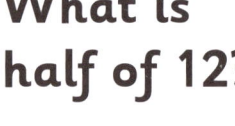

What is half of 12?

What is half of 10?

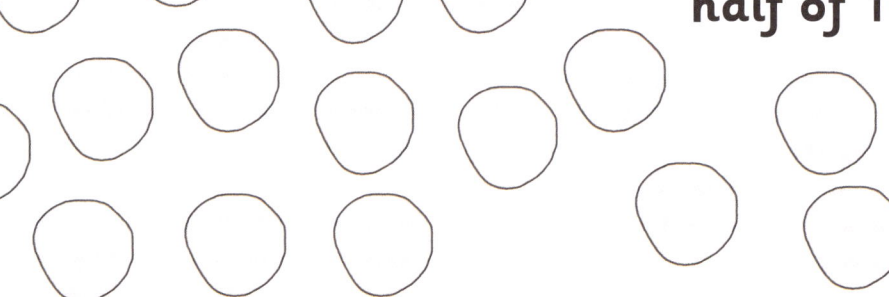

What is half of 16?

Answers on page 32

Test time!

Now you've worked through this workbook, test yourself on the following questions. Good luck!

3 + 7 = ☐   8 + 12 = ☐

Complete the following fact family:

● 3 + 7 = 10   ● ___ + ___ = ___

● ___ − ___ = ___   ● ___ − ___ = ___

Answers on page 32

Test time 2!

When you've finished, give yourself a reward sticker!

Keep going! You've got this.

Double 9 = ☐   Double 6 = ☐

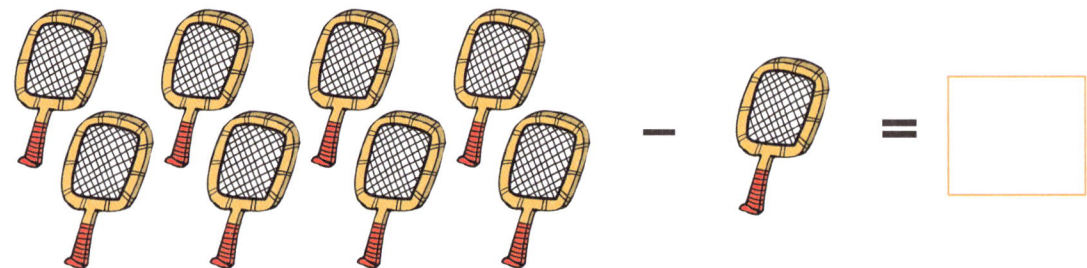 − = ☐

 −  = ☐

10 − 7 = ☐   17 − 6 = ☐

What is half of 14? ☐

Answers

Page 2-3: Counting 1 – 10
1, 2, 3, 4, 5, 6, 7, 8, 9, 10

Page 4-5: Counting 11 – 20
11, 12, 13, 14, 15, 16, 17, 18, 19, 20

Page 6: Adding one more
5 + 1 = 6   8 + 1 = 9
6 + 1 = 7   7 + 1 = 8
2 + 1 = 3

Page 7: Adding bigger numbers
2 + 3 = 5   3 + 3 = 6
4 + 3 = 7   4 + 2 = 6
5 + 4 = 9

Page 8: Number bonds to 10
6 + 4 = 10   3 + 7 = 10
8 + 2 = 10   9 + 1 = 10
5 + 5 = 10   7 + 3 = 10
4 + 6 = 10   2 + 8 = 10

Page 9: Number bonds to 20
13 + 7 = 20   8 + 12 = 20
14 + 6 = 20   9 + 11 = 20
15 + 5 = 20   10 + 10 = 20
17 + 3 = 20   18 + 2 = 20
1 + 19 = 20   12 + 8 = 20

Page 10-11: Super sums
4 + 3 = 7   5 + 4 = 9
2 + 6 = 8   7 + 4 = 11
9 + 5 = 14   7 + 8 = 15
1 + 19 = 20 2 + 8 = 10
7 + 7 = 14   6 + 9 = 15

17 + 3 = 20   10 + 3 = 13
13 + 4 = 17   2 + 9 = 11
4 + 11 = 15   3 + 5 = 8
15 + 5 = 20   7 + 12 = 19
4 + 6 = 10   13 + 6 = 19
5 + 4 = 9   12 + 5 = 17

Page 12-13: Fact families
3 + 7 = 10   7 + 3 = 10
10 − 7 = 3   10 − 3 = 7

1 + 6 = 7   6 + 1 = 7
7 − 6 = 1   7 − 1 = 6

5 + 4 = 9   4 + 5 = 9
9 − 4 = 5   9 − 5 = 4

5 + 8 = 13   8 + 5 = 13
13 − 8 = 5   13 − 5 = 8

2 + 3 = 5   3 + 2 = 5
5 − 3 = 2   5 − 2 = 3

6 + 5 = 11   5 + 6 = 11
11 − 5 = 6   11 − 6 = 5

Page 14: Missing numbers
3 + 4 = 7   6 + 2 = 8
5 + 4 = 9   6 + 5 = 11
6 + 10 = 16   8 + 10 = 18
12 + 3 = 15   14 + 2 = 16
5 + 13 = 18   8 + 11 = 19

Page 15: Seeing double
Double 3 = 6   Double 5 = 10
Double 6 = 12   Double 9 = 18
Double 7 = 14   Double 8 = 16
Double 4 = 8   Double 10 = 20

Page 16: Subtracting one
4 − 1 = 3   8 − 1 = 7
6 − 1 = 5   3 − 1 = 2
9 − 1 = 8

Page 17: Subtracting bigger numbers
9 − 3 = 6   8 − 4 = 4
6 − 4 = 2   7 − 2 = 5
9 − 2 = 7

31

Answers

Page 18: Subtracting from 10
10 − 7 = 3   10 − 4 = 6
10 − 3 = 7   10 − 8 = 2
10 − 5 = 5   10 − 2 = 8
10 − 6 = 4   10 − 1 = 9
10 − 9 = 1   10 − 10 = 0

Page 19: Super subtracting
17 − 6 = 11   18 − 5 = 13
19 − 4 = 15   17 − 3 = 14
16 − 5 = 11   14 − 6 = 8
12 − 5 = 7   13 − 7 = 6
15 − 8 = 7   18 − 9 = 9

Page 20-21: Fact families
9 − 7 = 2   9 − 2 = 7
2 + 7 = 9   7 + 2 = 9

8 − 3 = 5   8 − 5 = 3
5 + 3 = 8   3 + 5 = 8

9 − 5 = 4   9 − 4 = 5
4 + 5 = 9   5 + 4 = 9

13 − 8 = 5   13 − 5 = 8
5 + 8 = 13   8 + 5 = 13

10 − 3 = 7   10 − 7 = 3
7 + 3 = 10   3 + 7 = 10

11 − 2 = 9   11 − 9 = 2
9 + 2 = 11   2 + 9 = 11

Page 22-23: Subtracting superstar
6 − 4 = 2   9 − 3 = 6
17 − 4 = 13   19 − 5 = 14
14 − 8 = 6   9 − 8 = 1
19 − 9 = 10   15 − 8 = 7
10 − 7 = 3   15 − 9 = 6

16 − 4 = 12   11 − 2 = 9
12 − 7 = 5   13 − 6 = 7
15 − 7 = 8   17 − 9 = 8
15 − 5 = 10   16 − 7 = 9
14 − 6 = 8   19 − 6 = 13
15 − 4 = 11   12 − 4 = 8

Page 24-25: Subtracting from 20
20 − 7 = 13   20 − 4 = 16
20 − 9 = 11   20 − 6 = 14
20 − 5 = 15   20 − 14 = 6
20 − 12 = 8   20 − 17 = 3

20 − 18 = 2   20 − 13 = 7
20 − 8 = 12   20 − 16 = 4
20 − 2 = 18   20 − 19 = 1
20 − 1 = 19   20 − 11 = 9

Page 26: Amazing subtracting
8 − 6 = 2   6 − 5 = 1
19 − 8 = 11   17 − 3 = 14
14 − 8 = 6   17 − 9 = 8
15 − 8 = 7   20 − 13 = 7

12 − 5 = 7   15 − 9 = 6
17 − 7 = 10   18 − 13 = 5
17 − 15 = 2   14 − 7 = 7
19 − 9 = 10   18 − 10 = 8
16 − 13 = 3   12 − 6 = 6

Page 28: Halving
Half of 8 = 4   Half of 12 = 6
Half of 10 = 5   Half of 16 = 8

Page 29: Test time!
4 + 1 = 5   5 + 4 = 9
3 + 7 = 10   8 + 12 = 20

3 + 7 = 10   7 + 3 = 10
10 − 7 = 3   10 − 3 = 7

Page 30: Test time 2!
Double 9 = 18 Double 6 = 12

8 − 1 = 7   6 − 4 = 2
10 − 7 = 3   17 − 6 = 11

Half of 14 = 7